Next Church.Now

Creating New
Faith Communities

Craig Kennet Miller

D1025879

DISCIPLESHIP RESOURCES

P.O. BOX 340003 • NASHVILLE, TN 37203-0003
www.discipleshipresources.org

Other books by Craig Kennet Miller

Baby Boomer Spirituality: Ten Essential Values of a Generation
Encounters With Jesus: A Group Study in Baby Boomer Spirituality
Postmoderns: The Beliefs, Hopes, and Fears of Young Americans (1965 –1981)

Video

Now Is the Time: Ministry With the Millennial Generation (1982–1999)

Books coauthored by Craig Kennet Miller

Contemporary Worship for the 21st Century: Worship or Evangelism? (with Dan Benedict)
Culture Shifts: A Group Bible Study for Postmodern Times (with Lia Icaza-Willetts)

Reprinted August 2001, October 2000

Cover and book design by Sharon Anderson

Edited by Linda R. Whited and Heidi L. Hewitt

ISBN 0-88177-293-3

Library of Congress Catalog Card No. 99-068755

DR293

Contents

Acknowledgments

This book is the result of the influence of many people of faith who have challenged and encouraged me in my spiritual journey. Teachers such as Charles Kraft, Peter Wagner, Colin Brown, Roberta Hesteness, and Eugene Peterson have shaped my understanding of the church.

In my six years at the General Board of Discipleship, leaders such as Ezra Earl Jones, Karen Greenwaldt, Dan Benedict, Sang E. Chun, Roger Swanson, Lia Icaza-Willetts, Shirley Clement, Dan Dick, and many others on the staff have given me new tools for seeing the church of the future.

Leaders of new and existing churches, such as Nancy Woods, Rob Weber, Joe Connely, Dick Wills, Leo Hsu, Adam Hamilton, Michael O'Bannon, Kathy Townley, Vance Ross, Mike Pearson, Dick Freeman, Bau Dang, and Junius Dotson have given reality to the ideas expressed in this book. Clinton Parker, Eli Rivera, and Roger Patterson, colleagues at the General Board of Global Ministries, have also contributed to my thinking. Thanks also goes to the editors and producers of Discipleship Resources. My wife and daughter, as always, have given me great support.

The idea for this book germinated during a Sunday-morning Bible study at Belle Meade United Methodist Church in Nashville. Bruce Kauffman, the teacher for the day, laid out a history of the church in Ephesus, as seen in passages of the Bible from The Acts of the Apostles through the Book of Revelation. When I heard that history I said, "That's it." Bruce's lesson that day gave me the outline for this book.

Bruce works for the state of Tennessee in the agricultural division. He is a self-taught Bible teacher who has a passion for the ministry of leading a weekly Bible study at his local church. In many ways, Bruce, this book is yours.

Patmos, A.D. 90–95

I know your works, your toil and your patient endurance. I know that you cannot tolerate evildoers; you have tested those who claim to be apostles but are not, and have found them to be false. I also know that you are enduring patiently and bearing up for the sake of my name, and that you have not grown weary. But I have this against you, that you have abandoned the love you had at first. Remember then from what you have fallen; repent, and do the works you did at first.

(Revelation 2:2-5)

Introduction

A NEW WAY OF DOING CHURCH

At the core of the Christian spiritual journey is an awareness that God calls us to move forward, that we are to invite others to join us, and that the journey is one that is not to be walked alone. The early Christians were called "the Way." They did not see themselves as part of some kind of organized religion; instead, they were on an adventure of faith that compelled them to proclaim the grace of God to all who would hear. It compelled them to live out their faith in the midst of a community of faith whose primary mission was to witness to the world about salvation through Jesus Christ.

In countries around the world, new Christian faith communities that see their primary task as making new disciples of Jesus Christ are emerging. Today, new congregations are being formed that give people meaning, hope, and a place to call home. Even existing congregations are finding ways to open themselves to new people by creating new discipleship systems and new worship experiences.

The Primary Evangelistic Strategy for the Twenty-First Century

Key to this movement of the Spirit is the concept that conversion happens in the midst of Christian conversation, that rather than an us-against-them approach, people come to faith in the midst of Christian community. The primary evangelistic strategy of the twenty-first century is the establishment of new faith communities that invite people to experience the grace of God through the practice of the Christian spiritual disciplines, through hands-on experiences of mission and ministry, and through the celebration of the Christian life in worship.

A faith community is created when a worship experience is tied to a discipleship system. A worshiping group without a discipleship system is not a faith community; it is simply a place to worship God. A faith community intentionally creates settings that link worship to discipleship and spiritual formation. The primary purpose of this community is to reach out to new people to offer them experiences of the grace of God that can transform them into disciples of Jesus Christ.

One local congregation may have multiple faith communities. I experienced such a congregation firsthand in 1979, when I was the youth pastor of the Los Angeles Chinese United Methodist Church, which was established in the 1890's. This older existing congregation had a faith community that consisted of the Cantonese-speaking people who had their own worship experience, Bible studies, prayer groups, and fellowship groups in Cantonese. Another faith community within the church consisted of the English-speaking members of the congregation. Their worship experience—as well as their Bible studies, prayer groups, and fellowship groups—was in English. An additional faith community in this church was generational and was made up of those who were twenty-five years of age and younger. They also had their own worship experience, small groups, and fellowship groups. While the overall local church was united in its core values and its mission to make disciples of Jesus Christ, its vision and ministry were lived out through multiple faith communities within the congregation.

In my second year at Los Angeles Chinese United Methodist Church, the congregation launched a new church thirty miles away for members of the congregation who were American-born Chinese. Because the church's leaders were able to identify the needs of this particular people group in their midst, they were able to start a whole new church, which grew out of their English-speaking and younger-generation faith communities.

Multiple faith communities are also likely to develop when a local church offers more than one style of worship experience. Churches that have more than one worship experience may have at least two faith communities without realizing it. Each worship experience probably has small groups and fellowship or instruction groups linked to it, because the same people participate in these together.

In a congregation that does not contain different language groups, it is sometimes harder to identify different people groups and the faith communities to which they belong. Churches that have only one worship experience usually have only one faith community, provided they have established a discipleship system that enables people to grow in their faith and discover their ministry.

Growing Congregations Create New Faith Communities

The premise of *NextChurch.Now* is that growing congregations are those that create new faith communities that are able to meet the needs of specific people groups in their local community. At the heart of these faith communities is a deep desire to share the grace and witness of Jesus Christ in a way that invites new people to join in the Christian spiritual journey.

Local churches that have lost their way are often ones whose congregations have increasingly insulated themselves from change. They are holding onto old structures that no longer work; they are tied to an us-against-them mentality; and they have lost the passion to minister to those who live outside their doors.

In Revelation 2:2-5, John conveys a message from Jesus about the church in Ephesus:

> I know your works, your toil and your patient endurance. I know that you cannot tolerate evildoers; you have tested those who claim to be apostles but are not, and have found them to be false. I also know that you are enduring patiently and bearing up for the sake of my name, and that you have not grown weary. But I have this against you, that you have abandoned the love you had at first. Remember then from what you have fallen; repent, and do the works you did at first.

These words to the church at Ephesus are instructive to us as well. It is not enough simply to go through the motions of faith or to try to maintain what we have. Ephesus, an established congregation, had about forty years of history, but somewhere along the way it had forgotten its reason for being. The church had become good at judging right and wrong and at identifying those who were false. The church had endured much in the name of Christ; but while they had a great love for God, the Ephesian believers, at this juncture in their journey, had lost their love for those who did not know Christ. They had forgotten what Christ had done for them. They had lost their passion.

Jesus' prescription for them is fascinating to contemplate: "Remember then from what you have fallen; repent, and do the works you did at first" (Revelation 2:5). What was it that the church in Ephesus "did at first"? On what foundation was the church founded? What caused them to become a congregation that challenged the spiritual and cultural forces of its time? What was the nature of leadership in this local church? These are just some of the questions that come to mind as we read the words "do the works you did at first."

Because the New Testament gives us about a forty-year history of the church in Ephesus, from its conception to its adulthood, we can compare the development of the church in Ephesus with the church today. *NextChurch.Now* includes a variety of tools and graphs to help you understand the world in which we find ourselves today. The goal of this resource is to enable you to create healthy, vital faith communities that are a blessing to all who are touched by their ministry.

In this book, I argue that the new way of doing church is really an old way, one that is discovered by looking at the life of the church before the Modern Age began. By discovering our roots, we will move from a *mechanistic* image of the church to one that is *organic*. We will examine an understanding of the Christian life that considers the whole person and creates support systems that enable individual believers to contribute to the spiritual life of the whole Christian community. Key to this understanding of the church and of Christian life is the conviction that the primary purpose of the local congregation is not to maintain itself but to create settings where people can come to faith and belief in Jesus Christ.

Designed for Leaders of New Churches and Existing Churches

NextChurch.Now is written to provide guidelines and a process for creating new faith communities. The information can be helpful to two groups of leaders. One group consists of leaders in existing congregations who are looking for ways to understand their current congregation while at the same time developing fresh ways to reach out to new people in their local communities. A second group consists of leaders who are developing brand-new local churches. New-church planters, denominational leaders who have responsibility for starting new churches, and leaders of existing congregations who want to launch new churches may be included in this second group.

Throughout this book, examples from new churches and existing churches are blended together. The key points of learning about the overall concept of creating new faith communities are common to both groups. By following the process, leaders of both groups will be able to develop strategies for rethinking their own ministries and for creating new faith communities that will reach out to new people groups.

Conceptually, this book is divided into four sections that describe a systematic process for creating new faith communities. Chapters One through Four are about the importance of starting with the people group for whom the new faith community is being formed. Chapters Five through Eight look at the internal dimensions of the local church, including the creation of a healthy core group, understandings about church structure, ways to develop a discipleship system, and suggestions about how to maximize the effectiveness of the different kinds of group settings present in the local church. Chapters Nine and Ten focus on creating experience-based worship and on learning what is required to launch a new worship experience. The Conclusion asks what success is in Christian ministry and proclaims the importance of keeping the focus of the faith community on the call of Jesus Christ to ministry.

The Appendix includes information about additional resources; tip sheets; survey forms; and reproducible graphs, diagrams, and worksheets. You may photocopy the reproducible pages (177–91) to use with your local congregation. Also, you are invited to go to the Web site (http://www.umcncd.org) to find updates.

Often, we think of the journey of faith as an experience of the individual; but, as we will discover, God calls us to travel together as a people, for it is in the interactions with others that we grow in faith and find our place of service in the community of faith. Perhaps the secret we have forgotten is that congregations who give themselves away are the ones who grow.

Chapter One

LEADERSHIP
FIRST

Ephesus, A.D. 52

After staying there for a considerable time, Paul said farewell to the believers and sailed for Syria, accompanied by Priscilla and Aquila. At Cenchreae he had his hair cut, for he was under a vow. When they reached Ephesus, he left them there, but first he himself went into the synagogue and had a discussion with the Jews. When they asked him to stay longer, he declined; but on taking leave of them, he said, "I will return to you, if God wills." Then he set sail from Ephesus.

(Acts 18:18-21)

The closest we can get to experiencing Paul's arrival in Ephesus in A.D. 52 is to take a walk down the Las Vegas Strip. On each side of the street are some of the largest hotels in the world. Each casino has its own motif, paying homage to its own gods and goddesses. At the Luxor you can experience the grandeur of ancient Egypt. At Caesar's Palace you see all the splendor of Caesar's Rome. In the MGM Grand you can walk on Dorothy's yellow brick road. At New York-New York you can't help but be amazed by the majesty of the Statue of Liberty, around which passengers ride a roller coaster through all the classic sites of New York City. In the *Legends* show you can see Elvis, Marilyn Monroe, and other icons of the celebrity culture come to life.

Not to be forgotten is what is at the bedrock of each casino: the desire to get people to part with their money, to lure them into an attempt to trick fate by hitting it big in that one moment of ecstasy when all one's problems seem to be solved by winning the million-dollar jackpot.

But Las Vegas is more than just a place to gamble; it is one of the fastest-growing cities in the fastest-growing state in the

United States of America. From 1990 to 1998, the population of the state of Nevada grew by forty-five percent, making it by far the fastest-growing state in the nation. At the heart of the growth is the experience-based entertainment juggernaut known as Las Vegas. Those who have not grown up in southern California may not realize the allure of Vegas. In the heart of the Los Angeles freeway system, billboards often beckon riders to flee the traffic and find true happiness in the lush spectacle of a Las Vegas casino. More than a business, the Las Vegas Strip promises an escape from the futile toil of this world.

The city that Paul entered around A.D. 52 was no less grand. Ephesus was the most important city in the Roman province of Asia Minor. A magnificent wide street ran from the harbor through the heart of the city. Lined with columns, temples, a library, and a theatre that seated 24,000 people, the marble street made a grand statement about the city's importance in the Roman world. Known as the temple-warden of the emperors, Ephesus was by Paul's time a center of the emperor cult, as it possessed three official temples. Alongside these were temples for Apollo, Hercules, Pan, Pluto, Poseidon, Zeus, and the Egyptian gods Isis and Serapis, just to name a few. Included in the eclectic mix was one other place of religious fervor: a Jewish synagogue.

But all this was dwarfed by the largest building in the Greek world, the temple of Artemis—one of the Seven Wonders of the World. Four times the size of the Parthenon in Athens, it boasted 127 columns, some rising to more than 60 feet in height. The goddess of Ephesus was not just a local deity. Diana was the Roman incarnation of the Ephesian goddess Artemis. Throughout the Roman world, coins have been found bearing the inscription *Diana Ephesia*.[1]

The Making of a Leader

Conversion and Call

As Paul entered the city of Ephesus, he was on familiar ground. Since his dramatic conversion on the road to Damascus, Paul had spent many years traveling throughout the eastern Mediterranean proclaiming the gospel of Jesus Christ. In Galatians 1 and 2, we are told of the early years of Paul's ministry. He first spent three years in Damascus. Then, after fourteen years of ministry around Tarsus, Paul arrived in Jerusalem where, in a private conversation with Peter, James, and John, he shared a revelation: Paul was to proclaim the gospel to the Gentiles, while Peter was to focus on the Jews. In Galatians 2:7-10, Paul tells us:

> On the contrary, when they saw that I had been entrusted with the
> gospel for the uncircumcised, just as Peter had been entrusted with
> the gospel for the circumcised (for he who worked through Peter
> making him an apostle to the circumcised also worked through me
> in sending me to the Gentiles), and when James and Cephas and
> John, who were acknowledged pillars, recognized the grace that
> had been given to me, they gave to Barnabas and me the right
> hand of fellowship, agreeing that we should go to the Gentiles and
> they to the circumcised. They asked only one thing, that we
> remember the poor, which was actually what I was eager to do.

It was at this meeting that Paul's call to minister to the Gentiles
was confirmed by the leaders of the church. With this mutual understanding, Paul became the first missionary whose main strategy was
to establish churches in key locations throughout the Roman Empire.

Because of his background, Paul was uniquely qualified for the
task of establishing new churches. As one of the Jewish Diaspora, he
had been born and raised in Tarsus, a commercial city in what is
now modern-day Turkey. Raised outside of Palestine, Paul could not
help but be aware of the religious and social customs of the Greek-
speaking Roman world. As a Roman citizen, he was free to travel
throughout the Roman Empire, and his rights as a citizen in many
cases protected him from harm.

But more importantly, Paul was a Jew. Although past scholarship
has suggested that the Hellenistic (Greek-speaking) Jews were out of
touch with the authentic Jewish beliefs and practices found in the
center of Judaism (Jerusalem), recent discoveries show otherwise.
Research has shown that Paul was not a Jew in Greek clothing, but
in fact was an authentic first-century Jew.

In his article "Paul the Jew" in the *Dictionary of Paul and His
Letters: A Compendium of Contemporary Biblical Scholarship*, W. R.
Stegner shows how Paul carried with him four aspects of his Jewish
background. First, rather than being raised as a Greek-speaking Jew,
Paul spoke Hebrew in his home and saw himself as a "Hebrew born of
Hebrews" (2 Corinthians 11:22). Although Paul was born outside of
Palestine, his family took great care to see that he was raised in his
faith. Second, Paul was a "Pharisee's Pharisee," who believed in the resurrection of the dead and carried with him an apocalyptic view of the
world that was shared by other Jews of his time. Third, he lived out of
a Jewish mysticism, which explains much about his experiences of
visions and signs during his ministry. Fourth, his writings and way of
thinking show that he was formally trained in the Judaism of his day.
Stegner states:

> Two striking observations emerge... The first concerns how well Paul fits into the first-century, pre-A.D. 70 (Palestinian) Judaism that we know from other sources. For example, the same combination of zeal for the Law, apocalyptic worldview and mysticism characterized the Qumran sectarians. While not an Essene, Paul stands forth as a devoutly religious Pharisee of the time. The second striking observation concerns how well the pieces all fit together into a harmonious whole.[2]

Thus Paul's mission to the Gentiles was a radical departure for a zealous man of the Jewish faith who was charged with arresting the early Christian believers in Jerusalem and Damascus. His call to preach to the Gentiles was not simply to replicate the faith of his childhood but to create a new community of faith with a new people who formerly had been outside the borders of acceptance. This could be done only under the guidance of the Holy Spirit and with the deep convictions Paul carried as a result of his relationship with Jesus Christ. Paul's conversion on the road to Damascus (Acts 9:1-19) was just part of a lifelong journey of faith that compelled him in the end to preach the gospel to the highest officials of the Roman Empire. Paul challenged those leaders to turn from being his people's enemies to becoming fellow believers in Jesus Christ.

By the time we meet Paul in Ephesus, he is an experienced church planter. In the middle of his second missionary journey, he makes a quick stop in Ephesus on his way from Corinth to Jerusalem. With him are Priscilla and Aquila, two people who will play a key role in establishing a new community of faith in Ephesus. Priscilla and Aquila are first mentioned in Acts 18:1-3:

> After this Paul left Athens and went to Corinth. There he found a Jew named Aquila, a native of Pontus, who had recently come from Italy with his wife Priscilla, because Claudius had ordered all Jews to leave Rome. Paul went to see them, and, because he was of the same trade [tentmakers], he stayed with them, and they worked together.[3]

When Paul first met this engaging pair in Corinth, he had just weathered some of his worst experiences of ministry. In 1 Corinthians 2:3, he says: "I came to you in weakness and in fear and in much trembling." So far his early efforts at starting new faith communities had resulted in frustration and persecution. In Athens he had met with great resistance. In Thessalonica he had to leave the newly established church because of the threat of persecution. The first people he came in contact with in Corinth were fellow tentmakers (Priscilla and Aquila), but even more important, they were fellow Christians who had weathered the storms of persecution in Rome.

Leadership and Collaboration

While it is easy to think that Paul was a lone ranger, who went into the world alone to conquer it in the name of Christ, it is important to realize that the establishment of these new faith communities was a collaborative venture. Throughout the New Testament, we can identify with some probability thirty-six of Paul's coworkers with nine different titles.[4] Among the most important of these are Priscilla and Aquila, who played leading and supportive roles in three of the key churches of the time: Rome, Corinth, and Ephesus.

Priscilla and Aquila not only welcomed Paul when he arrived in Corinth, but they also ministered to him in his time of distress. Their prayers and encouragement were key to Paul's ability to preach in Corinth, where he stayed for eighteen months before going to Ephesus. The fact that Paul took Priscilla and Aquila with him to Ephesus was no accident, for Paul knew the city to which he was going and was not about to try to start the work there on his own.

Near the end of his ministry, Paul referred to Priscilla and Aquila as his coworkers in Christ: "Greet Prisca and Aquila, who work with me in Christ Jesus, and who risked their necks for my life, to whom not only I give thanks, but also all the churches of the Gentiles. Greet also the church in their house" (Romans 16:3-5). By this time we see that Priscilla and Aquila had returned to Rome and were the leaders of a house church. It was probably in such a setting that Paul found them in Corinth.

Choosing the Right Leadership

Paul's first decisive choice in starting the new faith community in Ephesus was to put the right people in places of leadership. He did not simply grab whomever happened to be available at the time; instead, he brought with him two of his most seasoned and experienced coworkers—Priscilla and Aquila. These were people who had been tested and who knew how to share the gospel in the midst of a hostile environment. They knew how to welcome new people into the faith.

When Paul left Priscilla and Aquila behind in Ephesus, they had three important tasks ahead of them: First, they had to get to know the territory and determine if it was the right place to start a new faith community. Second, they had to learn about the cultural environment and the current belief systems of the people groups they sought to reach. Third, they had to identify the people groups that lived in the city, in order to understand who would be the most receptive to the gospel.

While at the outset this may sound like a simplistic summary of the couple's work, the establishment of a local church in Ephesus would have been doomed to failure without accomplishing these three tasks. The things that are done first in the creation of a new faith community set the tone and the mood of what the congregation will be like in the future. The first steps—the prayer life, the methods of sharing the faith, the gathering of the core group, the establishment of the first small groups, the first practices of spiritual disciplines, and the nature of the first worship service—make up the genetic code that will run through that congregation for the rest of its existence.

Generating a genetic code is the single most important thing in successfully starting a new church or a new worshiping faith community. The traditions, rituals, and practices with which the faith community starts will determine the nature of the community in the future. Paul's hard-won experience taught him that he needed the most solid, prayerful, God-seeking people he could find—Priscilla and Aquila—to work with him in establishing a foothold for Christ in Ephesus. He also saw that the preparation and knowledge they gained while he went on to Jerusalem (Acts 18:20-22) would be invaluable for the starting of this new work.

Make no mistake about it, without the dedication and wisdom of Priscilla and Aquila, the work in Ephesus would not have gotten off to a good start. Paul's first decision, the choice of leaders, was the most important. Bringing Priscilla and Aquila with him enabled the new faith community in Ephesus to have a solid foundation on which the rest of that ministry would grow. Together, Paul, Priscilla, and Aquila had the needed spiritual gifts and experience to start a healthy faith community that would spread the gospel throughout the whole region.

Leadership Follows God's Call

John tells us that the Book of Revelation is addressed to the seven churches (1:11). All these churches—Ephesus, Smyrna, Pergamum, Thyatira, Sardis, Philadelphia, and Laodicea—emerged from the first steps taken in establishing the church at Ephesus.[5] Paul's goal was not just to start *one* church; his vision was to share the gospel with as many people as possible. And Paul's call was not simply to create faith communities for people just like himself. If that had been his goal, he would have been content to create churches for Jewish

Christians throughout the Roman Empire. Instead, Paul took the radical leap of faith to create new faith communities that would speak to the needs and visions of those who were very different from him in upbringing and heritage. The ministry in Ephesus was just the beginning of a strategy to create many new faith communities that all had the same goal: to make disciples of Jesus Christ.

Paul's perspective was at once universal and personal. His purpose was to witness to all who would hear him. He wanted people from all walks of life and from all heritages and cultural backgrounds to hear the gospel in their own languages and in their own cultural contexts. In this way, they could know the fullness of the grace and life found through belief in Jesus Christ. But Paul's call was not simply to nurture piety in the lives of individuals. Rather, the apostle had in view the transformation of the whole world in the name of the one true God, who had sent Jesus Christ to die so that all people could be saved. By sharing the Word of God in a way that could be understood by individuals in their cultural context, he sought to create a Christian community that would challenge the principalities and the powers that oppressed people everywhere and would prepare believers for the life to come.

Paul's experience is instructive for us who seek to establish new faith communities in today's world. It prompts us to ask ourselves searching questions, such as:

- Who are the most gifted leaders in our congregations?
- Are these leaders in places of ministry that allow them to reach new people for Christ?
- Do we know the surrounding communities well enough to identify the types of people groups that reside in our neighborhoods?
- Do we understand the cultural context in which Christians and non-Christians live their daily lives?
- Do we have a passion for sharing our faith in a way that non-Christians can understand so they can make their own decisions about God?

These questions should go a long way toward challenging leaders in congregations to look beyond the doors of their churches and to strive to be in ministry with those who live in the surrounding communities. Paul's witness says that as Christians, we are called to go beyond our comfort zone, to understand how non-Christians think, so that we can live in such a way that we are witnesses to the grace and love of Jesus Christ.

1.1. Key Events in Ephesus

A.D. 52		
Spring:	Paul, Priscilla, and Aquila arrive	Acts 18:18-19
	Paul goes to Jerusalem	Acts 18:21-22
Summer:	Apollos arrives and is sent to Corinth	Acts 18:24–19:1
Fall:	Paul returns and preaches in the synagogue for three months	Acts 19:1-8
A.D. 53		
Winter:	Public ministry is launched in the hall of Tyrannus	Acts 19:9-10
	Churches are planted in Asia Minor over the next two years	Acts 19:10-11
A.D. 55		
Fall:	A riot is led by silversmiths of Artemis	Acts 19:23-41
	Paul leaves	Acts 20:1
A.D. 57	Paul addresses the elders of Ephesus at Miletus	Acts 20:13-38
A.D. 62–66	Timothy pastors the church	I & II Timothy
A.D. 81–96	Revelation's message is sent to Ephesus	Revelation 2:1-7

Endnotes

1 See "Ephesus," by C. E. Arnold, in *Dictionary of Paul and His Letters: A Compendium of Contemporary Biblical Scholarship*, edited by Gerald F. Hawthorne, Ralph P. Martin, and Daniel G. Reid (Downers Grove, IL: InterVarsity Press, 1993), pages 249–50.

2 From "Paul the Jew," by W. R. Stegner, in *Dictionary of Paul and His Letters: A Compendium of Contemporary Biblical Scholarship*, edited by Gerald F. Hawthorne, Ralph P. Martin, and Daniel G. Reid; page 509. © 1993 InterVarsity Christian Fellowship of the U.S.A. Used by permission.

3 This reference to the Jews having to leave Rome had to do with a decree by the Roman Emperor Claudius in A.D. 49, as reported by Suetonius, in *Lives of the Caesars*: "Since the Jews constantly made disturbances at the instigation of Chrestus [*impulsore Christo*], he expelled them from Rome." (From "Claudius' Decree," in *Hellenistic Commentary to the New Testament*, edited by M. Eugene Boring, Klaus Berger, and Carsten Colpe; page 328. © 1995 Abingdon Press. Used by permission.)

4 See "Paul and His Coworkers," by E. E. Ellis, in *Dictionary of Paul and His Letters: A Compendium of Contemporary Biblical Scholarship*, edited by Gerald F. Hawthorne, Ralph P. Martin, and Daniel G. Reid (Downers Grove, IL: InterVarsity Press, 1993), page 183.

5 See Revelation 1:11; Colossians 1:7; 2:1; 4:16. See also *Zondervan NIV Bible Commentary: Volume 2: New Testament*, edited by Kenneth L. Barker and John R. Kohlenberger III (Grand Rapids, MI: Zondervan Publishing House, 1994), page 485.

Chapter Two

WHO ARE YOUR PEOPLE?

Phnom Penh, Cambodia, 1997

At a gathering of Cambodian pastors in Cambodia, Meng Top, a former prisoner of war who had escaped to the United States of America and had returned for the first time to his native land, said to the gathering in Phnom Penh: "My hope and prayer is that we become the Cambodian Methodist Church. Our goal should be to spread the gospel of Jesus Christ to our people."

As we entered Phnom Penh at dusk, it looked like a scene out of Mel Gibson's movie *The Road Warrior*. Residents of the city were zooming by on any ingenious contraption that could be hooked up to a bicycle. Buggy-cycles, wagon-cycles, and truck-cycles were all creating a huge cloud of dust in their wake. Women wore scarves and facemasks to keep the dust off their faces. Children clung to their parents as they headed down the road. One young boy surfed on a plank of wood that connected his father's bicycle to an old wooden cart. His balance and courage had to be as good as any professional making the surfers' circuit; for if he lost his balance, he would fall into the midst of a hundred bikes careening down the hard dirt road.

Riding in a convoy of vans were a group of Christian leaders from around the world. We were trying to determine the answer to one question: What was happening in Cambodia with the Christians called Methodist?

Representatives from the Singapore Methodist Church, the Korean Methodist Church, the United Methodist Central and Southern Europe Central Conference, the General Board of Discipleship, and the General Board of Global Ministries were gathering with a group of Cambodian refugees from Europe and the United States, who were taking us back to their native land to show us what Christ was doing in their homeland.

Each group had in mind a part of the picture of what was going on in Cambodia. The Singapore Methodists were starting an elementary school and a mission in Phnom Penh. The Korean Methodists had started a mission and a number of new faith communities throughout Cambodia. The central conference representatives had started a couple of local churches in Phnom Penh and the surrounding countryside. The refugee pastors from the United States had started congregations and house churches in the countryside. But no one in the group knew the whole story.

Cambodia is a land that is broken and bleeding from years of war. Our visit took place a couple months before the summer coup of 1997, in which one premier ousted the other premier in a series of political moves and pitched battles that spread from Phnom Penh to the border with Thailand. As we traveled, we saw the signs of the ravages of war that had torn the country apart since Pol Pot's rule. During the reign of Pol Pot (1975–1979), more than two million people out of a population of seven million were killed. For ten years, all the schools had been closed and thousands had fled the country.

One monument to the genocide told the horrible story. At the entrance to the Killing Fields stood a huge tower in which were stacked the skulls of thousands of people who were murdered under the regime of the Khmer Rouge. The refugees said that the first to be killed were those who were educated. The next were those who had any connections to the former regime. Last to go were those born from 1946 to 1965. Whereas Hitler had decided to try to kill a race, Pol Pot had decided to kill off a generation. His goal was to raise up the youth and children of Cambodia under his rule so that they would be loyal to him.

As we looked at this awful monument, one of the Cambodian pastors who had fled to the United States said, "I should have been here." Later he told how he had been in a prison camp for four years and had escaped during the last days of the war. He knows that God saved him, and he now serves a Cambodian congregation in the United States.

Our four-day journey was filled with discoveries of how God was moving among the Cambodian people. By the end of the week, we had discovered more than thirty churches that had been started in the last five years, primarily by the Cambodian refugees.

One story out of the many tells of the faith of these people. In 1978, after the Khmer Rouge had taken power, San Vorn was identified as a former policeman in the city of Phnom Penh. He and a number of other Cambodians were rounded up. San remembers how he stood in a line as the soldiers placed plastic bags over their heads and wrapped ropes around their necks. As a soldier came up to him, San remembered a missionary's words that encouraged him to believe in Jesus Christ. As the soldier tormented him, San prayed, "God, please save me. If you save me, I will use my life to follow Jesus."

Later that evening, one of the soldiers sneaked up to him and led him away from the others. Without saying a word, the soldier let him go free. The rest of the Cambodians were executed that night. Later, San fled to the border with Thailand, where he lived in the refugee camps. He remembered his prayer and asked the missionaries to help him learn more about God. By the time he arrived in the United States, he had become a Christian. Later, he became the pastor of a Cambodian-speaking community of faith at Modesto United Methodist Church in California. But this is just the start of the story.

Years later, in the late 1980's, members of San Vorn's faith community visited his hometown in Svay Rieng, about a four-hour drive southeast of Phnom Penh and close to the Vietnamese border. During their visit, they shared the Christian faith with their family members. One of those who listened intently was Sovandy Sok, a teacher in a local high school. After the visitors left, Sovandy wanted to learn more about Jesus Christ. He got a Bible, read it through many times, and then decided he wanted to be a Christian. But there was no local church in his community and few churches in the whole country, as Buddhism was the dominant religion.

When Sovandy's father-in-law saw his growing faith and his desire to be part of a faith community, he donated land to Sovandy so that a church could be built. The day after they registered the land, an attacker came into their home, held a gun to Sovandy's head, and threw him to the ground. Then the attacker aimed the gun at Sovandy's father-in-law and shot him dead. Sovandy fled as far away from the city as he could go.

In spite of his terrible ordeal, Sovandy did not lose his faith. Eventually, he made his way back to Phnom Penh, where he entered a Bible school so that he could become a pastor. When things calmed down in his hometown, he returned. With the help of the Modesto United Methodist Church, a congregation was established in Svay Rieng and a church building was built on the land of Sovandy's father-in-law.

When I met Sovandy, he was still attending Bible school in Phnom Penh. Every weekend he serves two house churches on Saturday and the church in Svay Rieng on Sunday. After the last service, he rides four hours on a motorcycle to go to school in Phnom Penh and then returns home again on Friday afternoon.

One of the most amazing experiences during our time in Cambodia took place when we visited the church in Svay Rieng. After a long journey, we came to a break in the road and drove on top of a dirt embankment that divided two rice paddies. After about a mile's drive, we came to a large clearing where more than 150 Christians greeted us. Next to the clearing was a beautiful building, complete with a fishpond and a well for fresh water for the community. There was much joy as we greeted one another in the name of Jesus Christ. Through a long thread of faith and belief on the part of people who once had not heard of Jesus Christ, a new faith community had been born.

Called to Be in Ministry With a People

In talking with the Cambodian pastors who had come to the United States, one thing was clear: They consistently referred to themselves as "a people."

As we think about the North-American landscape and the communities of faith that we are part of, do we have any concept that we are part of a people? Or are we a bunch of individuals going about our own tasks with the hope that not too many people will get in our way?

In the book *How the Irish Saved Civilization: The Untold Story of Ireland's Heroic Role From the Fall of Rome to the Rise of Medieval Europe*, Thomas Cahill tells the truly amazing story of Patricius, a sixteen-year-old boy who had been raised in Britain, but who now found himself a slave in Ireland. The slave of a shepherd, Patricius toiled in isolation in Irish fields, where in the midst of his anguish he learned to pray. One night a mysterious voice said to him, "Your hungers are rewarded: you are going home.... Look, your ship is ready."[1]

Trusting the voice, which he knew came from God, Patricius walked about two hundred miles to the sea. There he found a ship that was being loaded. After being denied passage, Patricius prayed again. Just as the ship was ready to sail, the captain relented and let him go aboard. After three days of sailing, they landed on the continent, only to find the area devastated by war. The year was probably A.D. 407, when the barbarians from the North were laying waste to the Roman Empire. When no food could be found, the captain of the ship challenged Patricius to pray for food before they all starved.

Patricius replied, "From the bottom of your heart, turn trustingly to the Lord my God,...for nothing is impossible to him. And today he will send you food for your journey until you are filled, for he has an abundance everywhere."[2] The sailors, worn out from hunger, bowed their heads to pray. Just as they tried out this newfound faith, a herd of pigs came running at them. Their hunger was satisfied!

After returning to Britain a few years later, Patricius was welcomed with open arms by his parents. Finding it hard to settle down, Patricius had a rough time in his homeland. He could not get the Irish out of his mind. Increasingly, he received visions from Christ to return to the Irish. One day he could not hold back anymore. He left Britain to go back to Ireland, where he became Saint Patrick, apostle to the Irish nation.[3]

This story is instructive because Saint Patrick, who by all rights would never want to return to Ireland, found compassion for the immortal souls of the Irish people and returned to share Jesus Christ with them. The British-born boy became the most celebrated Irishman of all time because he adopted the Irish as his people. In the midst of his suffering, God gave him a passion for witnessing to those who had enslaved him. Only God could melt the heart of one so abused, so that he could live out the rest of his days preaching the gospel throughout all of Ireland.

Saint Patrick's story echoes that of Saint Paul, the Jewish Pharisee who became the apostle to the Gentiles. Both Patrick and Paul adopted another people as their own.

In all three of these examples—the Cambodian refugees, who longed to see their homeland come to Christ; the British Patrick, who became the missionary to the Irish; and Paul the Jew, who became the missionary to the Gentiles—we see a common passion that fuels their vision for ministry: They are called to be in ministry to a people.

What Is a People?

What do I mean by "a people"? To start with, when you are part of a people, you believe that your future is linked to their future. A people group has a shared history and hope. Common goals, fears, beliefs, and vision link the members of the group. For individual members, belonging to a people group is a lifelong association; it is not something they jump in and out of on a whim. Those who belong to a people group have a vested interest in one another's welfare. Their values and beliefs are sustained through a network of relationships that give their lives meaning.

A people group may be a racial group, an ethnic group, or even a generational group. It also may be a community of faith, where there is such a deep sense of connectedness that all who are part of it share in one another's joys and sorrows.

In 1 Peter 2:9-10, Peter describes a new relationship with God that is found through belief in Jesus Christ:

> But you are a chosen race, a royal priesthood, a holy nation, God's own people, in order that you may proclaim the mighty acts of him who called you out of darkness into his marvelous light.
> Once you were not a people,
>   but now you are God's people;
> once you had not received mercy,
>   but now you have received mercy.

When a church views itself as a place where individuals get their own needs met, the church loses a sense of community. In a world where more and more people groups bump shoulders over many issues, Christian faith communities can become places where God forges a new people who love, care, and give in the name of Jesus Christ.

Throughout the biblical narrative, from Abraham to Moses and from Jesus to Paul, God calls leaders to share the faith with a people group. It is not enough for an individual to accept God and then worship God in isolation. What matters is how we live out the faith together.

It makes a difference when a faith community sees itself as a people. When the pastor of a local church sees the congregation as his or her people, and when the congregation accepts the pastor into their midst, God begins to move. Even more critical to becoming connected to a people is that the congregation sees itself as called to be in ministry outside its doors—in the community in which it lives. Suddenly, strangers are "one of us." They are our people.

The biblical imperative to reach out in ministry is found in the reason we are called to be God's people: "in order that you may proclaim the mighty acts of [God] who called you" (1 Peter 2:9).

Who Are Your People?

On the last night of our journey to Cambodia, Meng Top, a Cambodian refugee who had returned to his homeland for the first time since he had fled in the 1970's, said to the group: "My hope and prayer is that we become the Cambodian Methodist Church. Our goal should be to spread the gospel of Jesus Christ to our people." Meng's passionate plea was not to just preach in order to save souls or to minister to the needs of his family who had been left behind in Cambodia; his plea was to spread the gospel of Jesus Christ to his people.

As you think about your faith in Jesus Christ, a critical question to ask is, Who are your people? And an even more important question is, What people has God called you to call your own?

Key to the evangelistic enterprise is a spiritual leader, such as Paul or Patricius, who is called to a people. Is your congregation simply a conglomeration of individuals, or is it a people called by God to serve its community in the name of Jesus Christ? Is your local church a combination of people groups that are united by common core values and mission, or is it competing entities tearing the church apart?

The answers to these questions will tell much about your congregation's ability to grow spiritually and numerically in the coming years.

Endnotes

1 From *How the Irish Saved Civilization: The Untold Story of Ireland's Heroic Role From the Fall of Rome to the Rise of Medieval Europe,* by Thomas Cahill; pages 102–3. © 1995 Thomas Cahill. Used by permission of Doubleday, a division of Random House, Inc.

2 From *How the Irish Saved Civilization: The Untold Story of Ireland's Heroic Role From the Fall of Rome to the Rise of Medieval Europe,* by Thomas Cahill; page 104. © 1995 Thomas Cahill. Used by permission of Doubleday, a division of Random House, Inc.

3 See *How the Irish Saved Civilization: The Untold Story of Ireland's Heroic Role From the Fall of Rome to the Rise of Medieval Europe,* by Thomas Cahill (New York: Doubleday, 1995), pages 105–106.

Chapter Three

A MOBILE POPULATION

Pasadena, California, 1924

A five-year-old girl is invited by her grandfather to sit in the front of the church while he preaches in Swedish at the Pasadena Swedish Covenant Church. She listens intently to his words but understands little, as her language is English. She and her brothers are the first of her family to be born in America.

Family trees are all the rage. Computer programs and online services help people discover their lineage. Recently, I was surprised by one of my relative's investigations. With my aunt's Christmas card was a family tree that showed the Miller line going all the way back to before the Revolutionary War. Even more surprisingly, the first Miller of my family to make it to America came from Ireland. I had always thought that *Miller* was a variation of the German *Müller*. My aunt had also sent information about the Miller homestead in Pennsylvania. When I called the homestead to find out more information about it, the operator answered with these words: "Welcome to the home of the Whiskey Rebellion." You never know what you will find when you start examining your family tree!

In the last couple years, much has been made of the increase in immigration into the United States of America. From 1971 to 1993, more than fifteen million legal immigrants came into the United States. By 1994, 8.7 percent of the resident population was foreign-born. But this is nothing new. From 1901 to 1920, more than fourteen million people immigrated to the United States. By 1920, more than fourteen percent of the United States population was foreign-born.[1] Whereas most recent immigrants have come from Asia, Mexico, Central America, and South America, immigration at the beginning of the twentieth century came mostly from Europe.

It is hard to imagine it today, but during the early years of the twentieth century, native-born Americans complained about the "undesirables" from Norway, Sweden, Ireland, Italy, and the Slavic regions of Europe. These new immigrants brought with them their languages, food, dress, and cultures. Many wondered if these people were "real Americans."

It was during the period of immigration at the turn of the twentieth century that my grandfather and grandmother on my mother's side came to the United States. When my Norwegian grandfather arrived in 1906, he knew no one, nor did he know English—he was on his own. Traveling from New York, he arrived in San Francisco, where he worked in sweatshops as a tailor. After the 1906 earthquake, he moved to Everett, Washington, where he met and married my Swedish grandmother. On the surface, this marriage may sound somewhat tame, but for its time it was radical. In 1905, Norway had won its freedom from Sweden, and there was no love lost between the two countries.

By 1919, my grandparents had moved to Pasadena, California, and their families from Scandinavia had joined them. My Great-Grandfather Lungren was a lay preacher and a builder. After arriving in Pasadena, he donated the land for the Pasadena Swedish Covenant Church. My mother remembers being asked to sit near her grandpa as he preached in Swedish, even though she did not understand a word he said. That church stands in Pasadena to this day, but not a word of Swedish will be heard there. All the services are in English. Today, the challenge for this church is whether to start a worship service in Spanish or Chinese to meet the needs of new people groups that have moved into their community.

Population Growth Through Immigration

The state that has received the most new residents from outside the United States during this most recent wave of immigration has been California. In the 1980's, more than 3.5 million legal immigrants moved into the state. In the 1990's, this rate of growth has continued. Immigrants now constitute more than twenty-five percent of California's population and account for more than fifty percent of the state's population growth. Most of the new immigrants are younger than the statewide population, so one of the best ways to see the implications of the influx of immigrants is by looking at the population of college students.

In 1968, 91 percent of the freshman students at the University of California, Davis, were non-Hispanic white; 5 percent were Asian American; and 1 percent were African American. Mexican American was not even included as a category. In 1997, 43.7 percent of freshmen were non-Hispanic white; 27.7 percent were Asian American; 10.5 percent were Mexican American or Latino; 2.7 percent were African American; and 0.9 percent were Native American.

In 1998, about three out of every ten UC Davis undergraduates were born outside the United States. About half of all students came from a family that included at least one parent who was an immigrant. About one third of the students learned English as a second language.[2]

But immigration affects more than college campuses; it is also changing the makeup of cities across the United States. In Atlanta, new residents from China and Mexico are becoming part of a new ethnic mix that in the past was primarily black and white. In Omaha, Nebraska, a growing immigrant Mexican community has risen as farmers use their labor to produce their crops.

Immigrants and the New Hi-tech Economy

One of the effects of the growing hi-tech economy is the explosion of growth in the suburbs of major cities. Rather than the white flight of the past, the new formula of growth includes high-paying jobs in hi-tech industries and low-paying jobs filled primarily by immigrants with little education. Jobs such as gardening, childcare, and construction are filled by recent arrivals to the United States who are willing to work with their hands.

The suburbs around Washington, D.C., show this new growth pattern. Montgomery County, Maryland, and Fairfax County, Virginia, have experienced explosive growth from hi-tech industries. More than 3,300 hi-tech firms in the metropolitan area employ 250,000 workers. This economic change has been accompanied by a dramatic change in population. Approximately 500,000 legal immigrants have moved into the area since 1980, with perhaps an additional 250,000 illegal immigrants. What has changed from the past is that the new jobs and the new residents are concentrated far outside the urban center.

Fairfax County, Virginia, is home to America Online as well as a number of other Web site design firms. The county's population has nearly doubled since 1980 and is projected to reach one million by 2003. During that time, the non-white population increased at five times the rate as the population overall. The bulk of the newcomers were Latino and Asian immigrants. A 1996 study by the county government found that twenty-eight percent of the population had moved into the county since 1991, with one in five of the new-comers coming from overseas.

Not all recent immigrants filled low-paying jobs. In neighboring Montgomery County, the population experienced a 10.3-percent increase in the 1990's. A 1994 survey of the county found that in one out of four households, the head of the household or the spouse was born outside the United States. Nine percent of the foreign-born adults had a Ph.D., compared with six percent of the total population. But in neighboring Fairfax County in 1996, seventeen percent who had come to the United States in the last five years did not have a high-school education.

Immigrants to the total Washington, D.C., area show this same split. Recent immigrants are more than twice as likely to be employed as engineers or computer specialists as the native-born. At the same time, forty-one percent of recent arrivals hold jobs as food-service workers, janitors, and construction workers—jobs that make up thirteen percent of the total workforce.

In the information-age economy, suburbs are taking the place of urban cities as the port of entry for new arrivals into the United States. As a result, school systems that once served as magnets for whites leaving the cities face the challenge of educating the children of immigrants. In 1999, the Montgomery County's English as a second language (ESL) program served eight thousand students and was growing by five hundred new students a year.[3]

This new growth pattern is changing the dynamics of communities throughout the United States. In each case, churches in those communities are challenged to create new ministries to reach new people groups while at the same time trying to be in ministry to existing members. In many cases, a local church's future depends on its ability to create new faith communities for new people groups that have come into their community. Like the church in Ephesus, they have to be willing to bridge cultural gaps, in order to offer Christ to the new neighbors who are filling their communities. Today the mission field starts at the front door.

Population Growth Through Migration

Most people see immigration as the major factor in population growth in certain regions of the country, but this is only part of the story about population change in the United States. Migration of Americans from state to state is a major factor in population growth in some communities. Additionally, the migration of Americans from one region of the country to another is causing even more population change.

From 1990 to 1997, more than 88 million Americans moved from one county to another (35 percent of movers). Of these, more than 47 million moved from one county to another in their own state, while more than 40 million moved from one state to another. Additionally, more than 159 million (62 percent of movers) moved from one place to another within their own county.[4]

If a family moved from Pasadena, California, to Los Angeles, they would be staying within Los Angeles County. This counts as moving *within* one county. If the family moved from Pasadena (Los Angeles County) to San Diego (San Diego County), they would be moving from one county to another in the same state. If the family moved from Pasadena to Boston, they would be moving from one county to another county in another state.

3.1. Geographical Mobility of U.S. Residents Between March 1990 and March 1997

Total 1997 U.S. population: 262,976,000 Total movers 1990–1997: 255,150,000		
Residence	**Number**	**Percentage of Movers**
Different House in U.S.	247,297,000	97%
■ Same County	159,024,000	62%
■ Different County	88,272,000	35%
■ Same State	47,664,000	19%
■ Different State	40,610,000	16%

Compiled by the author from "Table A-4. Geographical Mobility by Tenure: 1986–1997," U.S. Bureau of the Census (http://www.census.gov/population/socdemo/migration/tab-a-4.txt).

Migration and a Shifting Population

The movement of population through migration has made some pretty remarkable changes in some states across the country. From 1990 to 1998, a dramatic growth took place in the West, with Nevada, Arizona, Idaho, Utah, and Colorado each experiencing a population growth of more than twenty percent.

Another group of states—Georgia, Washington, Texas, Oregon, Florida, New Mexico, North Carolina, Delaware, Alaska, Tennessee, Montana, and South Carolina—grew between ten and eighteen percent during the same period. Delaware, the only state in that group that is located outside the West or the South, grew by 11.6 percent.

Some states in the Northeast experienced a 2.2-percent or less growth in the same period: Massachusetts, Maine, West Virginia, Pennsylvania, New York, Connecticut, Rhode Island, and the District of Columbia. California, the most populous state in 1998 (more than 32 million), had a growth rate of 9.7 percent, which was close to the national rate of 8.7 percent.[5]

3.2. Map: Percentage Change in U.S. Population, 1990–1998

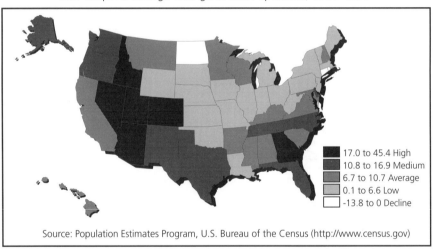

17.0 to 45.4 High
10.8 to 16.9 Medium
6.7 to 10.7 Average
0.1 to 6.6 Low
-13.8 to 0 Decline

Source: Population Estimates Program, U.S. Bureau of the Census (http://www.census.gov)

What exactly does all this information about the migration of the population tell us? It tells us that the American population is highly mobile. While we may look to overall population growth as a major change in local communities, a sometimes-overlooked factor is migration. In fact, if one adds up the number of people who made a move of residence of any type from 1990 to 1997, one discovers that 255,150,000 people moved. That is almost equal to the total United States population in 1997 of 262,976,000!

Of course, these figures do not tell us how many people made multiple moves during that period, nor how many stayed in one place; but I think you get the picture. People in our society are highly mobile, and a large percentage now find themselves living in a totally new community from the one in which they grew up.

A look at the growth of the top ten cites by percentage and by population gives us a more complete picture. Phoenix, Arizona, and its suburb, Chandler, experienced explosive growth in the 1990's. Chandler added 70,467 during this period. Combined, Phoenix and Chandler had an addition of 280,516 people. That number alone would have made it the sixtieth largest city in the United States in 1998, putting it ahead of cities such as Newark, New Jersey; St. Paul, Minnesota; and Louisville, Kentucky. Las Vegas, Nevada, and its suburb, Henderson, experienced similar growth, adding 233,180 people from 1990 to 1998.

3.3. Top Ten Cities—Percentage of Growth and Population Growth, 1990–1998

Top Ten Cities–Percentage of Growth, 1990–1998		Top Ten Cities–Population Growth, 1990–1998	
1. Henderson, Nevada	135%	1. Phoenix, Arizona	210,049
2. Chandler, Arizona	78%	2. Las Vegas, Nevada	145,411
3. Pembroke Pines, Florida	76%	3. San Antonio, Texas	137,616
4. Plano, Texas	72%	4. Houston, Texas	132,343
5. Las Vegas, Nevada	56%	5. Los Angeles, California	111,999
6. Scottsdale, Arizona	50%	6. San Diego, California	110,043
7. Corona, California	49%	7. El Paso, Texas	99,690
8. Laredo, Texas	43%	8. New York, New York	97,602
9. Coral Springs, Florida	42%	9. Plano, Texas	91,601
10. Palmdale, California	37%	10. Henderson, Nevada	87,769
Based on "U.S. Census: Place and County Subdivision Population Estimates,1990–1998" (http://www.census.gov:80/population/www/estimates/citypop.html).			

Taking notice of this huge growth, the Desert-Southwest Annual Conference of The United Methodist Church has undertaken a huge task: the creation of seventy-five new churches by the year 2010. Using a formula of one United Methodist Church per 43,000 residents, seventy-five new churches would barely keep up with the population growth of Nevada and Arizona.

Notice that these projections take into consideration only past population growth. To keep up with future population growth, even more churches would need to be created.

But what about existing churches? They, too, have a challenge: to create new faith communities that enable the congregation to reach new people groups in their community. This new people group may be Spanish-speaking people from El Salvador, or may be New Yorkers or Texans. They may be younger Postmoderns moving into an urban core where housing is less expensive. They may be new retirees moving into a college town. Whoever the new people groups are, the existing churches in the area need to know. And through that knowledge, existing churches can plan to be in ministry to the new people in the community.

Migration and Ministry

We cannot go into a state-by-state analysis of migration at this point, but one thing is clear: Local churches cannot help but be affected by these shifts in population. This means that you had better pay attention to the movement of people into your community—whether you are in Mobile, Alabama; Bloomington, Minnesota; Syracuse, New York; or Boise, Idaho—because your future congregation will come from this movement. Not only do congregational leaders need to pay attention to the overall population growth, but they also need to understand who these people are.

Pastors need people like Priscilla and Aquila in the congregation to scout the territory in order to learn how the community is changing. Make no mistake about it, every community is undergoing some kind of change. The vast majority of communities are seeing population growth, but just knowing that more people are around is not enough. Even more important to the future viability of a congregation is the knowledge of which people groups are moving into the community.

One Congregation's Approach

One pastor discovered that people in his community stayed an average of four years or fewer. To minister effectively to this mobile population, his congregation adopted the following strategy for ministry: The congregation's goal was to help people move from being seekers to believers to disciples and then to missionaries within three years. This church learned an important reality about ministry today: Most people who become part of a local church will move to other communities within ten years or fewer. The day of depending on lifelong members is over. Instead, this congregation realized two important things: First, they had to reinvent themselves every four years; and second, their goal had to be making disciples of Jesus Christ, not lifelong members of a local congregation.

The reality of movement of people from one region to another requires thoughtful consideration on the part of congregations; for each time a person moves, she or he is without a faith community—even if the person was part of such a community in the past.

The Critical Question

Beneath all the numbers that have been presented in this chapter is a critical fact that is ignored at our own peril: <u>Congregations grow or decline according to their ability to create new ministry settings for emerging people groups to experience faith in Jesus Christ.</u> This was easy to see in the 1800's because as the nation moved West, the church moved with it. As settlers moved west of the Mississippi River, Christian leaders went with them and created new local congregations in locations across the country. Today, the movement of populations is a lot murkier because people are criss-crossing the nation as they seek work, education, family, and safety.

It *is* possible to start new faith communities even in the midst of what seems to be highly "churched" communities, because underneath the semblance of stability is the vast, restless movement of people from one community to the next. This movement affects not only individuals but also the local congregation's approach to ministry. Chapter Four will offer one way to understand how the migration of people affects individuals and congregations alike.

As you think about the movement of people in your community, ask yourself these questions:

- ■ What percentage of our congregation moves out of town each year?
- ■ What percentage of people in our community moves out of town each year?
- ■ Who are the new people groups moving into town? Are they different from the people in the congregation, or do they reflect the same cultural values?
- ■ Who will be in the congregation of this church ten years from now—that is, what people groups will be found in our congregation a decade from now?
- ■ What needs to be done today to begin to be in ministry with them?

Endnotes

1 See "The Foreign-Born Population: 1994," by U.S. Bureau of the Census (http://www.census.gov/population/www/socdemo/foreign/fbrpt94.html). See also "No. 5. Immigration: 1901 to 1993," in *The American Almanac 1995–1996: Statistical Abstract of the United States* (Austin, TX: The Reference Press, Inc., 1995), page 10.

2 See "The New Face of UC Davis," by Kathleen Holder, in *UC Davis Magazine*, Winter 1998, page 19.

3 See "Crossing the High-Tech Divide," by Roberto Suro, in *American Demographics*, July 1999 (Overland Park, KS: Intertec Publishing Company), pages 55–60.

4 Compiled by the author from *Table A-4. Geographical Mobility by Tenure: 1986–1997*, U.S. Bureau of the Census (http://www.census.gov/population/socdemo/migration/tab-a-4.txt).

5 Compiled by the author from "USA Statistics in Brief—State Population Estimates," U.S. Bureau of the Census (http://www.census.gov/stat_abstract/part6.html). Go to http://www.umcncd.org/nextchurch.html to find a complete listing of states and their growth.

Chapter Four

MINISTRY WITH NEW PEOPLE GROUPS

United States, 2020

By 2020, the American scene will have changed dramatically. Vast movements of people groups will have shaped the face of the nation. At that time, Hispanics will be the largest minority group; Baby Boomers will be retiring; and the Millennial Generation will have led us through a dramatic youth boom that created a new worldwide youth culture. Local congregations who learned to create new faith communities will be the ones who are able to meet the needs of large numbers of people looking for a new spiritual homeland.

Churches will flourish or flounder depending on their ability to be in ministry to new people groups that enter their communities. These people groups may be generational, racial-ethnic, language, or cultural groups. While much thought and consideration needs to be given to leadership, to the spiritual vitality of a congregation, and to the types of worship that are offered, congregations must first come to know the people groups to whom they are called to be in ministry.

By the year 2020, the North-American scene will have changed in many ways. Through immigration and new births, the racial-ethnic mix will have changed. Sixteen percent of the U.S. population will be Hispanic, making it the largest minority. Non-Hispanic whites will make up sixty-four percent of the population; non-Hispanic Blacks, thirteen percent; American Indians/Eskimos/Aleuts, less than one percent; and Asian/Pacific Islanders, six percent.

But that's not the total story. From 1995 to 2020, all the minority racial-ethnic groups will have experienced growth in numbers of more than 34 percent. The non-Hispanic Black population will grow by 34 percent; the American Indian/Eskimo/Aleut by 37 percent; the Hispanic by 91 percent; and the Asian/Pacific Islander by 133 percent. Only the non-Hispanic white population (at 7 percent) will have slower growth in numbers.

4.1. Changes in the Racial-Ethnic Mix, 1995–2020

Year	Total U.S. Population	Hispanic Origin	White	Black	American Indian, Eskimo, Aleut	Asian, Pacific Islander
1995	263,434	26,798	193,900	31,648	1,927	9,161
2010	300,431	40,525	203,441	37,930	2,336	16,199
2020	325,942	51,217	208,280	42,459	2,641	21,345
Percentage Growth from 1995 to 2010	14%	51%	5%	20%	21%	77%
Percentage Growth from 1995 to 2020	24%	91%	7%	34%	37%	133%
Percent of Total Population in 1995	100%	10%	74%	12%	1%	3%
Percent of Total Population in 2010	100%	13%	68%	13%	1%	5%
Percent of Total Population in 2020	100%	16%	64%	13%	1%	6%

Compiled by author from "No. 19: Resident Population, by Hispanic Origin Status, 1980 to 1994, and Projections, 1995 to 2050," U.S. Bureau of the Census, Current Population Reports, pages 25–1095 and pages 25–1104 and Population Listing 21, The American Almanac, 1995–1996: Statistical Abstract of the United States, page 19.
Hispanic/Latino: People of Hispanic origin may be of any race.
White is non-Hispanic white.
Black is non-Hispanic black.

One group that does not show up in the census figures is people who identify themselves as multiethnic. Multiethnics are people who belong to more than one ethnic group, such as Asian/White or Black/Hispanic. In two surveys I conducted in the Spring of 1993 and 1995, six percent of Postmoderns (born between 1964 and 1981) identified themselves as multiethnic.[1] This trend will undoubtedly increase for younger generations, so that by 2020 more than ten percent of the population will identify themselves as multiethnic.

Most people from Asia, Latin America, Mexico, the Caribbean, and Central America do not think of themselves as Asian or Hispanic or Latino. But when they arrive in the United States, they find themselves labeled as Asian or Hispanic. Instead of these broad categories, Asian and Latin immigrants identify themselves by their nationality: Chinese, Japanese, Mexican, Bolivian, and so forth.

Just as my Swedish and Norwegian grandparents did, many Asians and Hispanics are marrying people outside their own nationality. While still listed as Asian or Hispanic, the new family will be a blend of different cultures within one racial-ethnic group. These combinations will produce offspring who will be even farther removed from the national culture of their immigrant forebears.

Generational Shifts Shape American Culture

By 2020, the United States will be in the midst of two significant generational changes. Baby Boomers (born from 1946 to 1963 and ages fifty-seven to seventy-four in 2020) will be changing the face of retirement in the United States. Their retirement means that the number of people age sixty-five and over will almost double—from thirty-three million in 1995 to sixty-two million in 2025.[2]

Another generational shift will be seen as the Millennial Generation (born from 1982 to 1999 and ages twenty-one to thirty-eight in 2020) will have taken American society through a youth boom that will rival the size and scope of the youth boom of the 1960's and 1970's. Larger than the Postmodern Generation (born from 1964 to 1981 and ages thirty-nine to fifty-six in 2020), the Millennial Generation will set their eyes on changing the world.

4.2. Generations

Many different dates have been proposed to define birth dates of various generations. In this book, the generations are divided into eighteen-year groupings so that we can get a clear picture of each generation's size relative to other generations. Key events also help to define a generation.

GENERATIONS	BIRTH DATES	CHARACTERISTICS
GIs	1910–1927	Also known as Builders. The Depression and WWII shaped their values.
Pioneers	1928–1945	Also known as Silents. They have led social change in music and culture. The Korean War and the Civil Rights Movement influenced their young adult years.
Baby Boomers	1946–1963	Led by the high school class of 1964, they were shaped by the events in the 1960's and 1970's.
Postmoderns	1964–1981	Also known as Gen X and Busters. They were born right after the assassination of President Kennedy and are the first generation to live out of a Postmodern perspective.
Millennials	1982–1999	Led by the high school class of 2000, they will set the trends in the first two decades of the twenty-first century.

From 2000 to 2020, we will see a youth boom during which youth will create new music, new dress codes, new cultural trends. They will make decisions about morality, values, and beliefs that will shape the direction of the rest of the twenty-first century. By their sheer numbers, this generation will have a profound effect on the American and worldwide culture.

What we already know about this generation should get our attention. Besides being larger in numbers than previous generations, the Millennials raised in the United States will have grown up amid great diversity. By the time they reach adulthood, about eighteen percent

4.3. U.S. Generations in the Year 2000

AGES		MILLIONS
91+	**WWI**	1
73-90	**GIs**	20
55-72	**Pioneers**	38
37-54	**Boomers**	73
19-36	**Postmoderns**	68
1-18	**Millennials**	75
	Source: U.S. Bureau of the Census (http://www.census.gov)	

will have been raised by an unmarried parent, about thirty-five percent will go through their parents' divorce, and about forty-seven percent will grow up with both parents in the home.[3] As a result, "family" will have a lot more to do with relationships than with biology.

Besides exhibiting greater racial-ethnic diversity than previous generations, eighty-five to ninety percent of Millennials will have been born in the United States, while ten to fifteen percent will have been born outside this country.

The Millennial Generation will face many challenges as they learn to live with the reality of their own diversity while dealing with the radical changes brought on by technology. One of the challenges will be how to bridge the gap between the haves and the have-nots. But perhaps the greatest danger to Millennials will be the attitude of previous generations, who may view them as the enemy rather than as a generation who needs support and guidance. Susan Mitchell, writer of numerous articles and books on generations, says that her greatest concern is the possibility of a "teenage backlash." She says that too often she hears people ask what can be done *about* this new generation, instead of asking what they can do *for* or *with* teenagers.[4]

Both of these trends—the retirement of the Baby Boomers and the Millennial youth boom—will create huge movements of people. While Boomers will be moving to smaller residences and to retirement homes and villages, Millennials will be moving out of their parents' homes into apartments and houses. In between will be the less-numerous Postmodern Generation, who will be faced with the question of how to provide resources and support for the more-numerous Boomers and Millennials.

As stated in Chapter Three, both the migration and the immigration of people change the shape of ministry in a given community. From 2000 to 2020, local congregations will make it or break it, depending on how well they adapt to the changing scene in their communities.

Stages of Change: How Do People Move?

Stage One: Homeland

Rather than looking at these generational shifts from a global perspective, let's talk about what happens when people move and about the stages congregations go through as they seek to meet the shifts in population in their communities.

When families move, they experience significant change. Some families relocate within the same county. Let's call this moving around in one's "homeland." Friends and family view such a move as progress. Parents or children are only a short drive away. Family members can get together for family celebrations, such as birthdays and holidays. The cultural aspects of life stay pretty much the same. They can still listen to their favorite radio station on the way to work, follow their favorite sports teams, and eat at their favorite restaurant (although it may be a little farther away). They can still be part of the same local church, although, in many cases, relocating within a large county may also mean a move to another congregation.

People who have lived in the homeland up until the age of eighteen have a strong connection to the homeland. Much of their identity is tied to their homeland's language, food, cultural institutions, and geography. For them, all future lands in which they live will be judged against their homeland.

Stage Two: Displacement

People who move from their homeland to another land have a totally different experience. Let's call this experience displacement. The farther people move from their homeland, the greater the displacement they feel. Movement from one county to an adjoining county is not as radical a change as moving from one state to another state, or moving from one country to another.

When a person experiences displacement, he or she goes through a number of levels of emotion: First, there is a *longing for home.* When I moved from southern California to Nashville, Tennessee, I missed family members. I missed friends. I missed weird things such as listening to Vince Scully announce the Dodgers' baseball games on the radio. I felt a longing for home.

The second level of displacement is a feeling of *us-against-them.* During this stage, the things a person misses become even more amplified. Differences seem very clear. On this level, I found myself saying things such as, "Nashville drivers are much worse than California drivers" or "I wish Nashville had a decent Mexican restaurant." A reciprocal attitude also existed. When I talked to a native Nashvillian, I would be asked where I was from. On the local talk-radio station, people would speak about "those damn Yankees," who were messing up the town. These feelings of displacement are amplified even further when a person crosses national, racial-ethnic, or language barriers.

The third level of displacement has to do with *discouragement.* At this juncture, the whole family becomes involved. One of the common conversations among coworkers at the General Board of Discipleship who have moved to Nashville is about spouses or teenagers who wonder why they had to make this move. On this level, a person wonders if he or she made the right decision and if there will ever be a place for "me" in this land. People desire to make something their own.

The fourth level of displacement is *decision:* Am I going to stay or go back? It is at this point that displacement reaches a breaking point. You can take only so much frustration, anger, and disappointment. Staying in a constant state of displacement is damaging and unhealthy. You have to decide to move back home or adopt the new land as your own.

Stage Three: New Homeland

Those who decide to stay in their new land will try to make it their own using one of the two basic strategies. One strategy people try is to re-create their homeland. One sees this easily in large immigrant communities. For example, in Alhambra, California, there are huge complexes of Chinese restaurants, stores, and businesses all catering to Chinese immigrants. In these places, Chinese is the prominent language and signs in Chinese are on the front of stores. Chinese immigrants can have all their needs met without having to speak English. The same is true in Miami, where immigrants from Cuba have created their own Cuban communities.

But it is not only immigrants who do this. Those who migrate from one state to another often do the same thing. When I visited a friend and his family who had moved from Orange, California, to Portland, Oregon, I was surprised to find them living in a housing development that was almost an exact duplicate of the one from which they had moved. Those born in Oregon call this phenomenon Californication, for many Oregonians deeply resent the growing pop-ulation of Californians who are bringing with them the smog, traffic, and culture from which they supposedly were trying to escape.

The other strategy people try is to adapt to the existing culture into which they have moved. Rather than trying to duplicate what they left behind, adapters create a synthesis of the culture they left behind and the new culture. They learn to appreciate the culture of their new homeland, but in the process they also help to change their new home-land. To put it another way, when immigrants or migrants arrive in a new homeland, this new home is bound to change. The native Orego-nians are right: The newly arrived Californians are going to change the whole community. This change becomes even more apparent when the numbers of new immigrants and migrants are large.

Typically, the first generation of immigrants or migrants in a new place will try to re-create their homeland, while their children will adapt to the new culture. Thus a transplant from Chicago to Miami will root for his "Cubbies" when they play the Florida Marlins, while his son or daughter will cheer on the Marlins.

This change in loyalty holds even truer when the children are born in the new homeland. Again, this is particularly apparent in the case of immigrants, who experience an ever-widening gap between the culture of their original homeland and the culture of the new homeland in which they are living. In some ways, these immigrants are dealing with three homelands at once. In their memories they carry the homeland of their birth while in their daily living they live in their re-created homeland. But in their interactions with their children, they are challenged by the emerging culture in which their children are living.

This synthesis of the existing homeland and the traditions and values of the newcomers creates an emerging culture that changes the fabric of the whole community. In the Atlanta school system, more than fifty different languages are spoken in the homes of children who attend the schools. This diversity changes everything. Those who have lived in Atlanta for generations will have to learn to relate to the newcomers because as their children live with the children of the newcomers, a new cultural perspective will be born.

Stages of Change: How Does the Church Respond?

Stage One: Congregations Protect the Traditions of the Homeland

Local churches respond to population changes in their communities in different ways. Stage-one congregations draw their membership primarily from people who grew up and stayed in their original homeland. The primary mission of the stage-one congregation is to meet the needs of local long-term residents. The primary desire of stage-one homelanders is to protect their homeland from outsiders. They long to hold onto the traditions of the past and to maintain the rituals and patterns of living that have sustained them. Their hope is that newcomers will become like them and will follow their ways of living out the faith.

4.4. Stage One

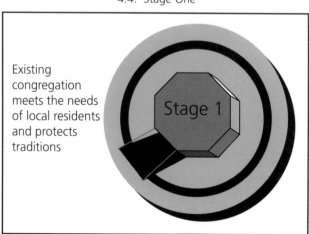

Existing congregation meets the needs of local residents and protects traditions

Stage 1

Stage Two: Congregations Live in Displacement

Whereas stage-one congregations try to protect what they have, stage-two congregations try to maintain what they have while offering hospitality to newcomers. Typically, they will respond to the changing community by sharing their facilities with a new people group. This type of response is commonly seen when an existing congregation opens its doors to a new immigrant group. The new faith community will meet for worship and education at a time and/or space different from the existing congregation. Conflict often ensues because the original group is trying to protect its original homeland and the new group is trying to re-create the homeland they left. Even though the two groups may try to learn to live with each other, they usually do not see the eventual synthesis of the two groups as the goal of this collaboration. A synthesis, such as having a joint worship service in English and Spanish, ends up making both groups dissatisfied.

While ideally we should all learn to appreciate one another's culture, the end result for a stage-two congregation is similar to the displacement one feels when moving to a new land—only in this case, both groups (the original congregation and the immigrant group) experience displacement. The original congregation sees a deterioration of its control and culture, while the immigrant faith community longs to have a place of its own.

The tension created in stage-two congregations comes about because what they are trying to create displaces everyone who is involved. As all the people groups try to maintain their own identity, they can end

4.5. Stage Two

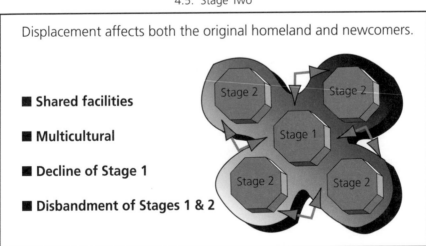

Displacement affects both the original homeland and newcomers.

■ **Shared facilities**

■ **Multicultural**

■ **Decline of Stage 1**

■ **Disbandment of Stages 1 & 2**

up in an us-against-them mentality. This mentality typically causes a sense of discouragement, with people in the original congregation asking, "Why did we allow them to come in the first place?" Or it causes the immigrant people group to ask, "Why do we want to stay here?"

In the end, stage-two congregations either decline or disband, because holding onto the tension between the multiple culture groups becomes untenable. One group wants to go back to the way it was in this place, while the other wants to create something that they can call their own. When the congregation's vision is simply to try to maintain an equilibrium between multiple groups, the congregation declines. The vision is not strong enough to hold the dream together. People groups long to have their own identity. This is no less true in a local church than in any other place.

This same conflict can be seen when new worship experiences are created for new people groups. For example, a generational group may desire a different kind of music than what the existing service (or services) offers. Usually, the new worship experience that is created is called an alternative service, which says to the newcomers that the new service is not the real service. As long as both people groups lack a common vision of belonging to the wider congregation, competition ensues and displacement is felt in both groups.

Stage Three: Congregations Create New Spiritual Homelands

Stage-three congregations create new faith communities by drawing from the emerging culture. Rather than trying to protect their homeland, stage-three congregations create new faith communities that speak to people who desire either to re-create their homeland or to create a new homeland. Successful new-church starts operate exclusively out of the stage-three mode.

A stage-three response can be seen in a congregation located in a new housing development. Such a congregation has no choice but to draw together a mix of people who have moved from a variety of places. In responding to the people in the new housing development, new local churches find themselves either re-creating the homeland of the dominant population or developing a brand-new model that grows out of the blend of people in the new housing development. The new development will look different from the development next door that was created twenty years before.

Whereas the established development is populated by people who have made this their homeland, the new development is an act of creation where a new mix of people from different backgrounds learn to live together. This difference becomes increasingly clear when their children end up going to school together.

Those who re-create the homeland of their people group will typically create an intergenerational racial-ethnic congregation that tries to closely model the traditions, worship styles, and culture of what was left behind. For example, a Korean congregation may offer a worship service in Korean aimed primarily at those who came from overseas and an English service for Koreans who were born in the United States. This re-creation of the homeland does not happen only in immigrant new-church starts. African Americans and Euro-

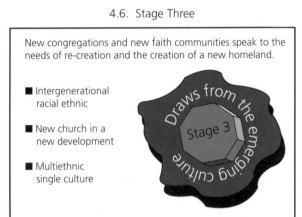

4.6. Stage Three

New congregations and new faith communities speak to the needs of re-creation and the creation of a new homeland.

■ Intergenerational racial ethnic

■ New church in a new development

■ Multiethnic single culture

Draws from the emerging culture

Stage 3

Americans often seek to create new faith communities that are duplicates of what they left behind, usually single-culture, single-race congregations. This practice is what has led some to say that the most segregated hour of the week is at eleven on Sunday morning.

Another strategy used in new congregations is creating a new faith community that emerges out of the new culture that is being created in the mix of people groups that are present in the wider community. Rather than being intergenerational, racial-ethnic congregations, they tend to be single-culture, generational churches. In Boston, I attended a new contemporary worship service in an existing congregation that met on Sunday evenings. For this group, race was not an issue. They were a multiethnic, single-culture faith community based on their generational group, which was primarily Postmoderns. This new faith community was focused on reaching a people group of a certain generation, rather than a race or ethnicity.

When most churches are started, they tend to reach a particular generation as the generation reaches its twenties and thirties. When we look at churches such as Willow Creek Community Church in Illinois or Saddleback Valley Community Church in California, we see two large congregations whose primary people group has been Euro-American Baby Boomers. Both churches are now seeing a need to create new worship services and ministries for Postmoderns. But in their inception they were primarily geared to a particular generation at a time when that generation was creating its new culture. Willow Creek was started in 1975, and Saddleback in 1980,[5] when Baby Boomers were graduating from college, getting married, and starting families. In many ways, both these churches have grown up with the Baby Boomers in their communities.

This reality is equally true of the church in which I grew up. My home church, which was founded in the 1940's as a spin-off from another Methodist church in Pasadena, California, has been a church primarily for the GI Generation (people who are now in their seventies and eighties). If you look at the history of your church, you will see that your congregation was created to meet the spiritual needs of the emerging people group of the time. In the case of my church, it was Euro-American GIs who had moved from the Midwest and had returned home from World War II.

Similarly, in the 1920's, the Swedish Covenant Church of Pasadena was started in order to meet the needs of Swedish immigrants and their families.

In each of these cases, the new congregation met the specific spiritual and cultural needs of the people group that was moving into its community. Years down the road, such a congregation appears to be a church for everyone; however, closer inspection reveals that the worship styles, congregational structure, group life, and cultural norms were set years before, when a new faith community was created to meet the specific needs of the new people group that was migrating or immigrating into the community.

Because a new faith community must meet the needs of a new people group, those who are called to minister to the younger Millennial Generation will need to seriously consider creating multiethnic, single-culture faith communities that reflect the current reality of the everyday life of these young people. A look at playgrounds and schoolyards in many communities will show an increasing multiethnic mix among the children and youth of today. A look in a local mall reveals a dating pattern that is multiethnic and signals to the observant church leader that a new faith community that is multiethnic will be critical for reaching this group of people.

Growing Congregations Start
New Faith Communities

One of the most important learning experiences I have had came when I moved to Nashville and started looking for a local church. I had never had to look for a church for myself. While I was growing up, I attended the local church my parents chose for me. When I was ordained as an elder in The United Methodist Church, I was appointed to the churches I was to serve. But in Nashville I had the opportunity to choose the congregation my family and I would attend.

It took us three years to find that place. Now, it would be easy to blame the churches we tried. But the truth is, it wasn't until I took part in helping to create a new faith community that I felt as if I had a spiritual home. When the church we had been visiting started a new worship service, I felt as if I had some part in its creation. My family and I were part of an experience of creating a new spiritual homeland.

Another myth that I realized isn't true is that people join a local church just because of the pastor. As one who pastored congregations, I usually took the credit or the blame for the level of growth or decline in the congregation. And I also felt that I was the major reason people joined or left. Maybe I felt that way because I had a big ego, or maybe it was because of my perception of what the church was about.

As I looked for a local church, I found that I wanted to be part of a faith community that welcomed me, cared for me, prayed for me, included me in its ministry, and challenged me to serve others. I became a part of the church I now attend because of the nature of the relationships within the faith community, not because of the pastor. To be sure, the pastor enhances what happens in the faith community and helps to create it, or the pastor can destroy the faith community if he or she is out of sync with the congregation. The pastor can create space for faith communities to grow and develop when he or she articulates the vision of how the congregation is to live out its faith and casts a vision for a better future. But in the end, people become a part of a community of faith when they choose to be on a spiritual journey with a group of believers.

Congregations who are reaching out effectively have leaders who help create the space in which multiple faith communities can develop and grow and have a life of their own. These multiple faith communities are a combination of small groups of from eight to twelve people and multiple worshiping communities. Each faith community speaks to the needs and concerns of a particular people group. Small-group ministries can form around the needs of particular groups of people in the community and in the congregation. These might be twelve-step groups, Bible study groups, church-school classes, musical groups such as choirs and praise bands. For many, these groups become their extended family.

The small groups come together as a worshiping community to celebrate their belief in God. When combined, the small groups and the worship experience become a faith community, through which people become mature disciples of Jesus Christ. A small group without worship is not a faith community. Conversely, a worship experience without a small-group system is not a faith community. It is a worship experience; it may even be called a church. But without a discipleship system made up of small groups, it is not a faith community, because a faith community sees as its role the developing and equipping of people for ministry. And without small groups, it is hard to develop healthy, mature leaders.

The Chinese Alliance Church in San Jose is a perfect example of this truth. They offer multiple worship experiences in a variety of languages that meet the needs of multiple people groups within the Chinese community. Worship experiences are offered in Mandarin, Cantonese, and English. Their newest worship experience is a youth service, which is an example of a generational, single-culture group in the midst of a larger Chinese congregation. This youth worship experience is combined with small groups to form a faith community. This new faith community has found its voice as it seeks to minister to a people group that shares a racial-ethnic heritage, the English language, a generational affiliation, and similar circumstances in life. It would be a waste of time to try to make the youth of that congregation attend the Mandarin or Cantonese service, because those worship experiences would not be able to speak to them in a language they understand.

But the people of the Chinese Alliance Church have not stopped there. They recently started a new youth worship and small-group experience on Tuesday nights called S.O.U.L. Fellowship (Shine On Us, Lord). This experience is geared toward youth of any ethnicity. Youth from the church invite friends to the service—friends who happen to be white, Black, Hispanic, or Asian. In this instance, an ethnically Chinese congregation is shifting its identity by reaching out through its youth to an emerging multiethnic people group made up of members of the Millennial Generation.

In the highly mobile society in which we now find ourselves, the most successful evangelistic strategy is the creation of new faith communities that speak directly to the newly emerging people groups living in the community surrounding local congregations. Rather than eliminating what they already have, growing congregations add new faith communities to their mix, making room for new people.

This strategy differs from the strategy of displacement. When we operate out of a displacement mentality, we try to keep everything the same while trying to tolerate the differences in others. The strategy of creating new faith communities also differs from that of stage-one congregations, which try to make everyone who joins the congregation like them.

Stage-three congregations allow for the possibility of change under the direction of the Holy Spirit. They make room for new people groups by creating multiple faith communities, while challenging the existing faith communities to grow and develop. Rather than trying to allot everything a specific place, the faith communities in the congregation intentionally learn from one another and allow new ministries to develop as the Holy Spirit calls them to ministry.

Christy's Experience

A number of people have become part of the new faith community that was created when Belle Meade United Methodist Church in Nashville started a new worship service. Recently, Christy, a twenty-five-year-old graduate student in molecular physiology, gave her testimony. Throughout her life she had viewed all the success she had as coming from her own talents and abilities. She had been a good student, athlete, and musician. After being in Nashville for a couple years, she heard about the new worship experience at Belle Meade and decided to try it out. She liked it and continued to visit.

One day, the leader of the praise band said they were in need of a keyboard player. When Christy heard the request, she felt certain that someone would step forward. But a couple weeks passed and no one did. So, after feeling a nudge from God, Christy told the band leader that she would give it a try. Her willingness to serve made a huge difference in her life. As she played the keyboard with the praise band, she became a member of a faith community who cared for her and taught her how to pray.

Each Sunday morning before the worship experience, the band gathered to pray. After a few times, Christy realized that everyone took turns praying, but she never did. She had never prayed out loud in front of others. For a whole week she agonized over what to say and practiced saying the correct words. When the praise band gathered to pray, she did it: She prayed out loud. It was a huge step of faith for her. Suddenly, she realized that all her talent came from God. It was a gift. Now her faith community is one of the most important aspects of her life. In the midst of Christian community, she discovered a whole new relationship with God and a new understanding of herself.

When the leadership of Belle Meade United Methodist Church started a new worship experience, they started something even more vital: They created a new faith community where people could explore their faith. As people came into the worship experience, they were invited to become part of small groups. The praise band became a new small group. The WWJD class was started for new Christians. A group of twenty-year-olds created a new small-group Bible study because all the Sunday-morning studies were populated by people in their thirties, forties, fifties, and sixties. Underneath the umbrella of the new worshiping community, small groups emerged that now meet the needs of new people who long to belong.

Christy, like millions of other people in America, was looking for a new spiritual home and a place to belong. She did not need to be confronted about whether she believed. In the midst of the worshiping community, she found acceptance and discovered that God had a place for her in the community of faith.

Congregations that will grow in the future are ones that create new settings where people like Christy can find their place and use the gifts God has given them. In communities across the United States, you will find churches that are growing. These churches share some common denominators:

1. They speak to the needs of emerging people groups in their communities.
2. They create new faith communities that are combinations of small groups and worship experiences that reach these people groups.
3. They release people to discover their gifts for ministry in the midst of the congregation and in the community.

Today, evangelism happens most effectively when new faith communities are formed to meet the needs of new people groups. It is that simple, and it is that complex. To succeed, most leaders and congregations have to rethink the way they do church.

Learning About People Groups Is Crucial

How does a congregation discover who the people groups are in its community? Cities, counties, chambers of commerce, and school systems often have this kind of information. Some universities and colleges will have a research department that may help. Another source of information is the U.S. Bureau of the Census (http://www.census.gov). Often, your denominational headquarters will have a research department.

Another helpful step is to fill out the "Community Profile" (page 177) and "Discovering People Groups" (page 178) worksheets. These tools will help you get a picture of your own congregation and community. You may want to ask the following questions as you look at the data:

1. What people group (or groups) did the congregation reach when it was first started?
2. What people groups are present in the current congregation?
3. What surprises about the makeup of the congregation did you discover?
4. Does the congregation mirror the mix of people groups in the community surrounding the church?
5. What people groups in the community is the congregation not reaching?

Endnotes

1 See *Postmoderns: The Beliefs, Hopes, and Fears of Young Americans (1965-1981)*, by Craig Kennet Miller (Nashville: Discipleship Resources, 1996), page 7.

2 Compiled by the author from "No. 17. Resident Population Projections, by Age and Sex: 1995 to 2050," by the U.S. Bureau of the Census, in *The American Almanac 1995–1996: Statistical Abstract of the United States* (Austin, TX: The Reference Press, Inc., 1995), page 17.

3 See "Children Born Outside of Marriage," by Ariel Halpern and Elaine Sorensen, in Urban Institute's *National Survey of American Families* (http://www.urban.org). See also *Postmoderns: The Beliefs, Hopes, and Fears of Young Americans (1965-1981)*, by Craig Kennet Miller (Nashville: Discipleship Resources, 1996), page 95.

4 Quote from Susan Mitchell given at the Millennial Generation Consultation, April 1998. Used by permission.

5 See *Baby Boomer Spirituality: Ten Essential Values of a Generation*, by Craig Kennet Miller (Nashville: Discipleship Resources, 1992), page 97.

Chapter Five

CORE VALUES FOR A CHANGING WORLD

Oxford, England, 1729

Mr. M[organ] told me he had called at the jail to see a man who was condemned for killing his wife, and that...he verily believed it would do much good if anyone would be at the pains of now and then speaking with them.... On the 24th of August, 1730, my brother and I walked with him to the Castle. We were so well satisfied with our conversation there that we agreed to go thither once or twice a week; which we had not done long before he desired me to go with him to see a poor woman in the town who was sick. In this employment too, when we came to reflect upon it, we believed it would be worth while to spend an hour or two in a week.

John Wesley[1]

While the change in demographics in a community may challenge a local congregation to be in ministry to new people groups, an even more profound shift is challenging the way we think about and understand the role and the purpose of church life.

There was a time when the local congregation served as the center of the social life of the community. The church was where transitional life events such as weddings and funerals took place. It was the place where one made business contacts and went to look for a future spouse. It was the place where children learned lifelong values and made lifelong friends. The church provided a place for church socials, Christmas parties, and the celebration of national holidays. It was at the center of the community's life. Much of what happened was cultural. Activities and events reinforced community values and shaped the world-view of the next generation.

Today, the role of the church has changed. Rather than being the cultural center of a believer's life, it is the spiritual center. It is the place where one taps into the core values of the Christian faith and learns how to be a Christian in a world that in many ways is hostile or, even worse, indifferent to Christianity. People do not desire more activity; instead, they long for purpose and meaning.

As a result, effective congregations are ones that focus on the core values of the Christian faith and center on teaching people spiritual disciplines that will last a lifetime. The focus is on spiritual formation rather than on knowledge.

As we will see, this shift in the role of the church has some profound implications for the way we do church and for the part the church plays in the believer's life. First, this shift highlights the difference between cultural norms and core values. Second, this shift forces us to look to the roots of the Christian faith to find new insights for today. Third, in light of the transition from the twentieth century to the twenty-first century, the shift in the role of the church causes us to rethink our church structure and the way we do our work.

Cultural Norms and Core Values

When we put the words *change* and *church* together, many legitimate and important questions are raised. Most of the confusion about change has to do with the difference between cultural norms and core values. Cultural norms and core values are not the same.

Cultural norms are things such as the dress code for worship, the type of music the congregation sings, and the style of the church building. In one local church, the leaders of the new worship service that met in the chapel wanted to place artificial plants around the altar to soften the look of the worship space. When word of this got out to the wider congregation, this group was told that artificial plants were not allowed in the church. If they wanted plants in the chapel, they had to use live plants.

Many churches go to war over issues such as this. The battles are, for the most part, over cultural norms. Neither the Bible nor denominational standards such as *The Book of Discipline of The United Methodist Church—1996* gives guidance about what kinds of plants are allowed in a local church. These are issues the local church decides according to the cultural norms and traditions of the people group the congregation is currently serving.

A congregation's cultural norms are fairly easy to see, especially for the outside observer. Additionally, these norms can easily be broken unintentionally by newcomers. When I went to serve as the pastor of a small rural church in southern California, I noticed that a red light was left on in the altar area of the sanctuary. Being a good steward, I turned off the light. The next morning I found myself in trouble with one of the members of the trustees because I had turned off the "eternal" light that had been given in memory of one of the past members of the congregation. Even though no one had told me about this tradition, I was to blame because "anyone with a brain" would have known that this was an eternal light. I'm sure it said so right on the package!

Cultural clashes such as these happen whenever some kind of major change takes place in a local congregation. When a new pastor comes to serve a church, when a new worship service is started, when a new people group uses a space usually used by another group, some kind of conflict often ensues. People take sides. In the past, the youth would be blamed; now it is the new Korean or Spanish congregation. You get the picture.

Core values, however, are the bedrock beliefs and purposes that guide a congregation's decisions. Many congregations make the mistake of thinking that what unites them are common experiences, such as having the same style of worship, the same time for church school, the same fellowship groups, and so forth. But these experiences are only the outward expression of something that goes much deeper. While many congregations may seem to be united because they all do the same thing, what really unites a congregation is having the same core values.

Each of us, whether we have pastored or been a member of a local church, can tell stories about the conflicts produced by cultural norms. These issues are part of the territory of church life. In 1 Corinthians 1:10-15, Paul points to this very fact:

> Now I appeal to you, brothers and sisters, by the name of our Lord Jesus Christ, that all of you be in agreement and that there be no divisions among you, but that you be united in the same mind and the same purpose. For it has been reported to me by Chloe's people that there are quarrels among you, my brothers and sisters. What I mean is that each of you says, "I belong to Paul," or "I belong to Apollos," or "I belong to Cephas," or "I belong to Christ." Has Christ been divided? Was Paul crucified for you? Or were you baptized in the name of Paul? I thank God that I baptized none of you except Crispus and Gaius, so that no one can say that you were baptized in my name.

Paul's solution to the problem was to help the people remember their call rather than to focus on whether they should follow him or Apollos. In 1 Corinthians 1:26-31, the apostle says:

> Consider your own call, brothers and sisters: not many of you were wise by human standards, not many were powerful, not many were of noble birth. But God chose what is foolish in the world to shame the wise; God chose what is weak in the world to shame the strong; God chose what is low and despised in the world, things that are not, to reduce to nothing things that are, so that no one might boast in the presence of God. He is the source of your life in Christ Jesus, who became for us wisdom from God, and righteousness and sanctification and redemption, in order that, as it is written, "Let the one who boasts, boast in the Lord."

Paul implored the people to go beyond their differences to see what united them. He pointed out the core values they all shared: God called all of them; none could boast, because they were all followers of Christ Jesus; in Christ they found righteousness, sanctification, and redemption.

Churches get themselves in trouble when they confuse core values and cultural norms. Core values remain constant while cultural norms vary from place to place and from time to time. When a congregation's core values and cultural norms are at odds with each other, the congregation has two options: First, the congregation's leaders can call people to adopt a new way of life, to take on the core values of the Christian life. Or, second, the congregation can become just like the society in which it finds itself, discovering its primary purpose in lifting up and maintaining the cultural norms of the culture.

Core Values, Mission, Vision, and Ministry

In recent years, many churches have worked to put together mission statements that seek to spell out their core values. But in many ways these efforts have fallen short because people have misunderstood the differences between *core values, mission, vision,* and *ministry.*

Using the image of a spaceship leaving the launching pad, let's explore these issues. Core values are the fundamental beliefs and experiences that form the Christian faith. One's faith, understanding of Scripture, experiences of God, and traditions all go toward forming core values. Core values form the filter through which we judge right and wrong, make choices and decisions, and evaluate our actions. A core value of the Christian faith can be seen in John 3:16: "For God so loved the world that he gave his only Son, so that everyone who believes in him may not perish but may have eternal life." Core values form the *launching pad* for our actions and practices.

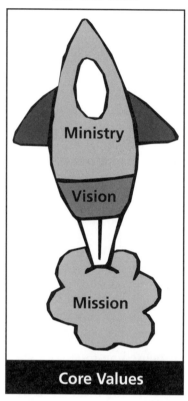

5.1. Core Values

The next important issue is mission. At its 1996 General Conference, The United Methodist Church stated its mission: "to make disciples of Jesus Christ."[2] Making disciples is what The United Methodist Church sees as its primary purpose for being. The mission is the *fuel* for what we do.

The mission, however, does not tell congregations how they should go about the task of making disciples—which brings us to the matter of vision. To accomplish the mission of making disciples, each local congregation must put that mission into action by capturing and articulating a specific vision for how the task will be accomplished. Vision is tied to understanding and speaking to people in the context of their cultural norms. Vision, therefore, changes according to the people group with whom a congregation is seeking to be in ministry. Vision is the *navigation system* that tells direction—where the congregation is going.

Ministry is the end result of all three: core values, mission, and vision. Ministry is the way a congregation lives out its core values, its mission, and its vision as its serves in the name of Jesus Christ. Mission is lived out in the strategies of ministry. Ministry is the *payload* that the congregation delivers, operates, and offers once it has arrived at its destination.

The Holy Club

In 1729, John Wesley found himself in a conflict between core values and cultural norms. When John came to Oxford, he found that his brother, Charles, had started a new faith community. John joined Charles and two other believers, and the foursome committed themselves to meeting on a regular basis to pray, to read the classic texts of the early church fathers, and to hold one another accountable for their actions. They also took Holy Communion once a week.

About six months later, the four friends were asked to speak to a man who was in prison for killing his wife. It was requested that they minister to the man before his execution. Later, they collected money to free people from debtors' prison. Soon they were the scandal of Oxford. They were called various names, including the "Holy Club," "Bible Moths," and "Methodists."

Three of these participants were to transform the nature of Christianity in England: John Wesley became the leader of the Methodist Societies; Charles Wesley wrote indigenous Christian music that changed the face of congregational worship; and George Whitefield became known as one of the greatest evangelists of his era.

In his journals, Whitefield talks about his experience of being part of the Holy Club:

> Whether I ate or drank, or whatsoever I did, I endeavored to do all to the glory of God. Like them...I received [the sacrament] every Sunday at Christ Church. I joined with them in keeping the stations by fasting Wednesdays and Fridays and left no means unused, which I thought would lead me nearer to Jesus Christ.... I was from time to time engaged to visit the sick and the prisoners, and to read to poor people, till I made it a custom, as most of us did, to spend an hour every day in doing acts of charity.[3]

Members of the Holy Club were deeply focused on their core values. Rather than living by the current cultural norms of the Anglican Church and British society, they examined the spiritual leaders and writers of the past. By immersing themselves in the Bible and in the writings of the early Christians, they discovered a new way of understanding the Christian life. Rather than the formal rigidity of the Anglican Church, the Holy Club came to understand the Christian life as relational. The mission of the Holy Club could be summed up in the phrase "love God and neighbor."

The core values and mission of the Holy Club led its members to a vision that moved them beyond simply taking care of their own needs to meeting the needs of those around them, even the most destitute and despised people in their society. But rather than being well received by those in the church and by fellow students and professors at Oxford, Wesley and his friends were mocked and laughed at; they also faced stiff opposition from many different factions. In spite of this opposition, these early Methodists held fast to their spiritual disciplines and, in time, changed the face of a nation.

Spiritual disciplines were a vital facet of this process of discovery and experimentation because the practice of spiritual disciplines forms and sustains the core values. John Wesley called the spiritual disciplines "means of grace." Through the practices of acts of justice and compassion, the public worship of God, the ministry of the Word, the Lord's Supper, family and private prayer, searching the Scriptures, fasting or abstinence, and Christian conferencing, the early Methodists developed a lived theology that moved them deeper into their love and understanding of God. As they practiced the means of grace, Wesley and his friends began to see the world through different lenses.

5.2. Wesley's Means of Grace

- Acts of justice and compassion
  (doing no harm and doing good)
- The public worship of God
- The ministry of the Word, either read or expounded
- The Supper of the Lord
- Family and private prayer
- Searching the Scriptures
- Fasting or abstinence
- Christian conferencing (conversation)[4]

John Wesley and the leaders of the Methodist movement discovered that the church of their day was not speaking in the language of the common people of England. The church was living on the basis of the cultural norms of the upper crust of English society and was not meeting the needs of the people who were facing crime, poverty, and violence on a daily basis. The genius of the members of the Holy Club was not only their ability to articulate and live out their core values, but was also seen in their mission and vision that enabled them to be in ministry to the people who surrounded them but were virtually invisible to the established church. The church's mission appeared to be directed primarily at those who were just like the people who were already in the church. The scandal of the Methodists lay in their willingness to reach out to a people group that was outside the church and that lived outside the confines of "polite" society.

The Church and the Modern Age

Today, we find ourselves in the midst of a shifting sea of cultural change and practice, in which it is hard to distinguish cultural norms and core values. For the last fifty years, much of the church has been wedded to a Modern understanding of the world, aligned closely with a Modern view of life. We find ourselves living in a postsecular, supernatural world, in which the values, beliefs, and norms of the Modern Age no longer apply.

The Modern Age started about 1901 and was built on the foundations of the European Enlightenment (eighteenth century). The Modern Age came to an end about the same time as the first landing on the moon (1969). A number of beliefs were common in the wider culture in the Modern Age. For example, they believed that truth is found through the scientific method. By using the five senses, human beings could discover what was true and what was false. Things that could not be proved by the scientific method were suspect. In this framework of belief, the existence of God could not be proved; indeed, neither the existence of God nor the reality of life after death admitted to scientific proof.

The environment of the Modern Age was hostile to many traditional Christian beliefs. For example, they did not believe that miracles happened. Healing took place because of the proper use of medicine, not because of prayer. Belief was more important than faith. Believers were people who adopted and followed a given set of beliefs that were logical and consistent. The battle over the inerrancy of the Bible turned on whether the Scripture met the test of the scientific method. Thus, either all of it was true, or none of it was true.

5.3. Secular Beliefs of the Modern Age

- Guided by reason.
  (John Locke: "Reason must be our last judge and guide in everything.")
- No miracles, just reasonable explanations.
- Spirituality is emotionalism.
- Jesus as a good example.
- Religion is well-ordered, codified, and authenticated by agreed-upon customs.
- Inspiration and vision are dangerous.
- Morality is based on personal preference.

Ministry in the Modern Age

One of the most significant ways in which Modern thinking has influenced the church is in the area of church structure: how the church organizes itself and how it views and carries out its ministry.

Central to the Modern Age is the notion of the *specialist*, who focuses all of his or her reasoning power on one aspect of life. Rather than affirming a holistic view of life that takes in a wide variety of information from many different sources, the Modern Age encouraged people to focus on their limited area of specialty, plumbing its depth to the virtual exclusion of all other areas of knowledge. For example, in the field of medicine, one doctor specialized on the heart while another focused on the brain; but they rarely talked to each other (as if the heart and brain did not reside in the same body). Fields such as sociology, anthropology, and psychology sought to apply scientific methods to the human condition, with each developing its own techniques, theories, terminology, and perspective on how humans function in the world.

Similarly, in the world of religion, ministry became more specialized as ordained pastors moved from being pastors to becoming professionals who did the ministry on behalf of the congregation. It was out of this specialization and professionalization of the ministry that a Modern structure of congregational ministry emerged. We will call this the twentieth-century system.

The church of the twentieth century rested its hope on reason. Buying into the perspective of the wider culture, it sought to prove the existence of God primarily though scientific means. It also adopted the Modern hierarchical structure of work that saw ministry as being primarily the job of the professionally trained ordained minister. The responsibility of the Modern pastor

5.4. Twentieth-Century System

Professional Ministry

Academic Preaching

Committees

Programs

was to do the ministry on behalf of, and in the name of, the congregation. He or she was to do the preaching and teaching, to visit people who were sick and people who were limited in their ability to leave home, and to attend all the meetings. Also, he or she was to preside at all weddings and funerals, as well as to lead worship and administer the sacraments.

Membership in the Modern Age

When the Modern church reached its zenith of power in the late 1950's, one of its key assumptions was that everyone in the community was a Christian believer or an adherent of another religion. In 1957, ninety-six percent of Americans claimed a religious affiliation.[5] In this context, the goal of the church was not so much to invite people to become Christians as it was to invite people to become members of a particular congregation. There were two basic ways for a congregation to assure that it was a notch above the rest: First, it had to have a better preacher than its peers. Second, it had to have more exciting programs. When evangelism did take place, it was through the use of tools such as the Four Spiritual Laws, which outlined a process for being saved. Evangelism was logical and progressive. Belief had to make sense, or else it was not true. Faith was rational and linear.

Preaching in the Modern Age

Preaching in the Modern Age was primarily academic. Its presentation was didactic, linear, and rationalistic. The preachers operated on the assumption that, because of their theological education, they knew more about the Christian faith than the congregation did. The congregation operated on the assumption that a good preacher was one who knew more than they did. The job was well done if the preacher delivered a well-thought-out sermon with three points and a good story that was logically presented so that everyone could agree or disagree. People could say, "Yes, I believe that is true." Whether people lived out the point of the message was irrelevant. What made it good was that it was believable.

A good sermon in the Modern Age would devote twenty minutes to the history of prayer in the Bible and one minute to personal application, which went something like this: "Therefore, go and pray." There was an assumption that, because everyone in the congregation was a Christian, everyone already knew how to pray. People just needed to be encouraged to do a better job of praying.

Programming in the Modern Age

The Modern church sought out more members by trying to provide the best programs in town. The church with the most active women's and men's groups, the best Sunday school, and the most-innovative youth group was considered superior. Everyone wanted to belong to that church. The church with the most people involved in its programs invariably would attract the most visitors and, as a result, would have the most members.

The goal of providing innovative and exciting programs, however, was not discipleship; the goal was membership—a place where you as a believer could belong and raise your children in the best Christian educational program available.

Leadership in the Modern Age

In order to run its programs, the church needed committees to organize and to plan for ongoing programs and events. Typically, the planning committee would meet at the beginning of the year to decide what everyone else was going to do for the rest of the year. Once the planning was done, the responsibility of seeing that the plans were carried out lay in the hands of the professional minister and the church staff.

This cycle of leadership was self-perpetuating because each segment fed the next: The pastor or a layperson would propose a new idea. A program would be designed to meet the need. A committee would be put together to supervise the program. Professional staff or the pastor would be charged with recruiting volunteers and running the program. The pastor would preach about the importance of everyone getting onboard with the new program. And, once started, the program was hard to stop. After all, everyone in the church said it needed to be done.

The Church at the End of an Age

But what happens when something goes wrong at a fundamental level, at a level much more profound than the failure of the preacher, the chairperson of the administrative board, or the new children's coordinator to do their jobs properly? What happens if the whole set of assumptions on which this Modern system is built no long rings true with the wider culture?

When people talk about the death of the church or the decline of Christianity, more often than not they are pointing to the package, not to the contents—the way of doing things, not the core values.

From generation to generation, the core values and beliefs of the Christian faith remain. What has changed is how and to whom it is being passed on.

The Church of the Twenty-First Century

Today, we find ourselves in a new world. Up until the 1980's, the predominant world-view of the twentieth century was Modern. In the last twenty years, we have gone through the Postmodern Age, during which many of the tenants and values of the Modern Age were challenged. But now we find ourselves in a Post-Postmodern Age. A new way of thinking is emerging that combines the sensibility of the Modern Age with the spirituality of the first century.

Postmodern thinking challenged the Modern view that scientific knowledge is superior to other forms of knowing. It went so far as to say there is no such thing as truth; truth is only what is good for those who are in power. We are aware of the limits of truth found through scientific means. For example, one week we are told that caffeine kills; the next week it is reported that people who do not drink caffeine are at a greater risk of committing suicide. The challenge to the superiority of scientific truth has moved people into a different way of finding truth. Today, people come to truth through a process of discovery rather than by adopting a set of beliefs. Scientific truth has a place, to be sure, but science does not have the final say. For something to be true, it has to be confirmed by personal experience.

During the height of the Modern Age, it was believed that through scientific means humanity would have unending, unlimited progress. During the 1960's, the space race seemed to confirm this dream. Through a series of amazing inventions and innovations, the United States was able to land a human being on the moon. Humanity seemed to have conquered nature itself.

But since the landing on the moon, events such as the Apollo 13 mission and the fear of weapons of mass destruction have caused people to ask if science has all the answers. And after the space shuttle Challenger exploded in 1986, many people came to the conclusion that the answer is no.

The Challenger disaster was a keystone in the minds of the Postmodern Generation (those born from 1964 to 1981)[6] because the vast majority of them viewed it firsthand. On that day, school children around the country were watching the launch live on televisions in their classrooms. During that whole week, NASA was going to beam the results of a number of scientific experiments into public-school classrooms. Onboard the shuttle was Christa McAuliffe, a schoolteacher from New Hampshire, who was selected to teach the nation's school children about the excitement of traveling in space. When the shuttle exploded soon after the launch, children and teachers around the nation were in shock. Drilled into their consciousness was the message that science does not always come out all right. Scientists make mistakes.

The Challenger disaster was for Postmoderns what the assassinations of the 1960's were for Baby Boomers: the death of a dream and a questioning of all the assumptions that went with it.

A New Way of Seeing the Truth

As the Modern view of science was put on the chopping block, the issue of what is truth became a point of contention. The question about truth is not so much about whether there is any truth as it is about how one finds and confirms the truth. Saying a person has to experience something first before believing it to be true is not much different from the scientist saying that only statements confirmed by scientific methods are true. The difference lies in the kind of filters one uses to determine the truth.

The Postmodern perspective caused people to look for expanded models of how to find truth and how to live life itself. Today, people are more apt to look to the past for ways to find truth than to try to imagine the future. This back-to-the-future perspective provides the church with an exciting opportunity to draw on its own past for a model of knowing and living. John Wesley, whose ministry took place in the 1700's, proposed a way of knowing and experiencing God that is equally applicable to us. Let's call it Wesley's filter.

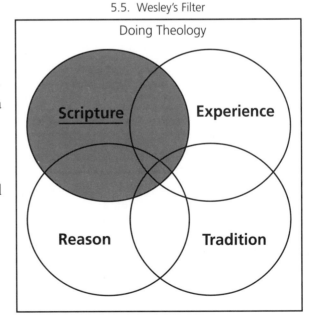

5.5. Wesley's Filter

Doing Theology

Scripture

Experience

Reason

Tradition

Wesley said that we come to understand God through four primary ways: First, we are empowered by God through the *Scripture*. Scripture is the bedrock of the Christian faith. The shared stories, accounts, wisdom, and commands of the biblical narrative form the foundation on which our core values are built.

Second, we discover God through *experience*, which confirms for us the validity of the Bible's truth-claims. Experience also enables us to touch base with our heart-language and the images that connect us to the emotions and feelings of life. The joy of holding a newborn child is not as much an event that is confirmed by our reasoning as it is an encounter that transforms the way we will experience life in the future.

Third, we find God by listening to and learning from the *traditions* of our faith. Tradition consists of the shared experiences, practices, and wisdom of the Christian community passed on from generation to generation. The validity of tradition is found in the stories and accounts it contains of how God has touched the lives of people who lived before us. New meaning and insights come as one touches base with the traditions of Christian people. Those new meanings and insights in turn give new meaning to what we experience today.

Fourth, we use our *reasoning power*. We think, we reflect, we ask questions—and we seek truth with our minds.

A New Way of Viewing the World

The twenty-first century brings cultural shifts that will virtually change the way people perceive reality. The way we spend our time, with whom we spend our time, how we process information, where we live, and to whom we can and do communicate is drastically altering the world in which we live.

The next ten years will continue to push the limits of what is real, what is true, and what is ethical. While Postmodernism has been good at pointing out the flaws in Modern thinking, it has not been good at pointing us toward a common vision and common understanding of the world in which we live.

The engine that has fueled the dramatic changes of the last twenty years has been the digital revolution built on the back of the microchip, which is found in almost every electronic device we have at our disposal. With the development of each new digital-era device, new ways of communicating and interacting have taken place.

In the summer of 1998, I saw how dramatically things had changed. For the last four years, I had given leadership at the School of Congregational Development that was held in the summer. From 1994 to 1998, we held the school on the campus of Boston University, where participants were housed in dorms. Each year there was a battle over the phones. Since there were no phones in the rooms, everyone had to share a common phone. In 1998, the phone was not installed in time for the start of school, so participants were anxious about being in communication with their family and churches back home. After two days, the phone was put in place. When I came out of my room to see how things were going, people were lined up at the phone holding their personal computers. They didn't want to call anyone, they wanted to check their e-mail!

In a few short years, the Internet and e-mail had changed the way these pastors were doing their work and the way they were communicating. Twenty years from now, people will look at the way we communicated at the end of the twentieth century the way we now view horse and buggies as a means of transportation at the end of the nineteenth century.

Today, it is a common experience for my third-grade daughter to interact with a variety of media that were not available or even invented twenty years ago. Instead of watching a television program, she more often watches her favorite video on a VCR. Instead of listening to a record, she plays a CD. Instead of typing on a typewriter, she uses a word-processing program on her computer.

Some say that by the time my daughter is a teenager, a hand-held device will be available that will be a computer, television, camera, fax machine, e-mail device, and telephone rolled into one. Instead of carrying this device, my daughter will more than likely have it imbedded in her clothes. Instead of typing into this device, she will talk into it as it turns her spoken words into written words that can be e-mailed to her cousin in Los Angeles. Or she can use the device to have a face-to-face, two-way video conversation with her cousin.

My daughter will be able to do this whether she is in Nashville, New York City, or Mexico City. It won't matter where she is because the worldwide satellite system will transmit live media no matter where she is on the globe. More than that, my daughter will have her own identification number (similar to a social security number), which will also serve as her phone number, her e-mail address, her medical identification number, and her credit-card number. Using this technology will be so simple that information will flow as easily as it does when you are standing face-to-face in the same room with a friend.

A New Way of Working

This fusion of technology and lifestyle is moving people into a new way of working together. It is not just the way we live our lives that is being changed; the way we interact, the way we organize, and the systems we use to accomplish goals are changing as well. As a result, a number of differences in work styles can be identified—with important consequences for the church, as we will see.

First, one person cannot do it alone. One person cannot keep up with all the changes and understand all the issues. It takes a team of people working together to make things happen.

Second, no one person has all the expertise or knowledge. What is important is the shared knowledge of the organization.

Third, change is not going to slow down. Structures created today will be good for about six months to two years. Organizations that are flexible and smart enough to be constantly reinventing themselves are the ones that thrive in this new environment.

Fourth, organizations as well as individuals have to become lifelong learners. Through constant learning, organizations are able to anticipate, update, and work with change.

Fifth, stability is not based on structure; instead, it is based on the nature of relationships. Is there mutual trust? Are individuals encouraged to grow and expand both spiritually and in their area of expertise? Does everyone win when one person wins? Do organizations focus on the development of people and release them to do the work they are called and gifted to do?

Sixth, the organizations with the most creativity will be the ones that are the most adept at interacting with the culture in ways that can make a difference. What counts is not static knowledge or expertise; what makes a difference is the ability to adapt quickly to changing circumstances.

Seventh, character and integrity count. People become part of an organization because they trust the leadership.

5.6. A New Way of Working

1. There are no lone rangers.
2. Knowledge is found in the group.
3. Change is not going to slow down.
4. Learning is a lifelong process.
5. Stability is based on the nature of the relationship, not on structure.
6. Creativity wins.
7. Character and integrity count.

These seven points have important implications for the church. For one, congregations in the twenty-first century need to be safe places where the leadership has the trust of the people and where individuals can explore their faith. Congregations of the twenty-first century need to be willing to learn and to change, in order to meet the needs of a changing culture.

Recently, I talked with Jeff Spiller, pastor of Christ United Methodist Church in Mobile, Alabama. He is the founding pastor of the church that is now twenty years old. I asked him how many churches he has served. He told me that he has served five different churches, but they all had met in the same location for the past twenty years! What Jeff meant is that as his church has grown and developed over the years, he has had to grow and develop along with it. Every four to five years, Christ Church has reinvented itself as it has grown and reached new people in the community. Today, it is not the same church it was when it started. If the church hopes to continue to be effective, it will have to be a new church four years from now, too.

A New Way of Being Church

These new assumptions and shifts point to a different way of understanding the role of the church and what it is to be about in the twenty-first century. The changes that are shaping our world provide an opening for the church to affirm afresh the core values of the Christian faith.

Affirming core values means that rather than a mechanistic view of the congregation, leaders take an organic view of the church. Rather than focusing on one element, they look at the whole system. Rather than talking about religion, they focus on the spiritual journey. Rather than finding people to fit into a particular spot in the church structure, they create a structure that fits the call of the one who seeks to be in ministry. God is not dead; God calls all baptized believers into ministry.

As a result, congregations who are living out of this new reality take a different approach to how the church should structure itself for ministry and how it should carry out its ministry in the world. This new approach is radically different from the way many churches approached these issues in the twentieth century. Let's look in more depth at some of the implications of this thinking for the church's structure and ministry.

Ministry of the Baptized

Instead of viewing ministry as the work of professionals, effective congregations in the twenty-first century will operate out of the belief that *all* the baptized are called to be in ministry. Rather than allowing an antagonistic division between clergy and laity, all believers will be seen as being called into ministry. Some people have particular gifts and are called into the ordained ministry, but that limits neither the responsibility nor the gifts of all the other believers in the congregation. Everyone is equally called and gifted for a particular ministry.

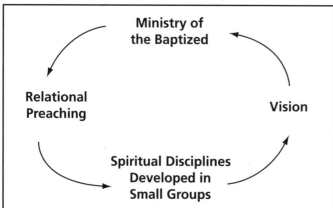

5.7. Twenty-First-Century System

Ministry of the Baptized

Relational Preaching

Vision

Spiritual Disciplines Developed in Small Groups

Preaching in the Twenty-First Century

Instead of assuming that everyone is a Christian and knows how to live out the Christian lifestyle, people who preach in the twenty-first century will use a set of assumptions different from those of the Modern Age. Today, a majority of people in the wider society are not active in a local church. Many have never been taught the basics of prayer, reading the Bible, fasting, worship, or doing acts of mercy. The goal of preaching in this context is to instruct and teach people how to live out the Christian faith in the midst of a rapidly changing world. This instruction is relational. Preaching discusses real-life issues and communicates by talking about the experiences of faith and practice that shape core values. It focuses on the heart. Thus, the majority of the time in a sermon on prayer would be spent on a theme related to application, such as "Does God Listen When You Pray?" or "Developing a Daily Prayer Life."

An even more vital goal of preaching is to articulate the mission and cast the vision of what a community of faith is to become as it seeks to be faithful to God's will. Core values, mission, vision, and ministry are brought, through the preaching ministry, to the forefront. The goal of preaching is to help the listeners see the connection between the core values (the Scripture for the day) and their ministry (the way they live out the core values in daily life). Academic preaching was content to stop at the core values. Relational preaching challenges and gives handles on how to live out these core values in ministry.

Church Structure in the Twenty-First Century

Churches that understand the dynamics of change do not plug people into ready-made programs. Instead, visitors, participants, and members are invited to gather in small groups where they learn to live out the spiritual disciplines of the Christian faith. Together they hold one another accountable and challenge one another to grow in faith. As they pray, study the Scripture, and seek God's will, vision for ministry begins to arise.

In these churches, committees do not meet to decide what the rest of the congregation is going to do for the rest of the year. Instead, the ministry of the baptized responds to God's call for ministry and sees the vision for ministry that arises out of small groups and individuals as they practice and reflect on their spiritual disciplines. Once

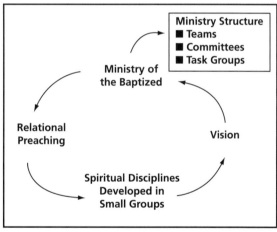

5.8. Structure for the Twenty-First-Century Ministry System

Ministry Structure
■ Teams
■ Committees
■ Task Groups

Ministry of the Baptized

Relational Preaching

Vision

Spiritual Disciplines Developed in Small Groups

a vision for a particular ministry is articulated, the leadership works in partnership with the individual or small group to discern the kind of structure that needs to be put into place to make the ministry happen. Is this ministry best done by a task group, a team, a committee, or by some other means? Structure is created and designed to give feet to the vision.

Leadership in the Twenty-First-Century Church

The role of the congregation's leadership is not to say no. Rather, the role of leadership is to set guidelines and boundaries and to put into place structures that will enable new ministry to bear fruit.

Dick Wills, senior pastor at Christ United Methodist Church in Ft. Lauderdale, Florida, provides these simple rules of thumb for ascertaining God's call about a potential ministry. To become a valid ministry at Christ Church, a new ministry must meet one of the following criteria:

1. It introduces people to Jesus in positive ways.
2. It disciples believers through Wesley Fellowship Groups (Christ Church's small-group discipleship system).
3. It relieves suffering.[7]

If the proposed ministry does not meet one of these simple criteria, then it's back to more prayer and reflection.

While ministry happens in both the twentieth-century and twenty-first-century church systems, what is different is the starting and ending points. In the twentieth-century model, the starting and ending points rested with the professional staff. In the twenty-first-century model, the starting point is vision as it arises out of the prayers of the whole body of Christ. The ending point is the empowerment by the whole body of Christ to do the ministry.

At Christ Church, Dick Wills and his staff do not have to dream up new things for the congregation to do. Instead, these leaders watch and let ministry occur naturally as God works in the lives of the baptized.

The beauty of this approach is that as new ministries arise, the congregation's structure changes with them. Rather than trying to force the new ministries to fit old church structures, the leaders empower ministry to unfold as it is unveiled in God's timing.

Empowering the Laity

Christ Church's approach contains a critical element that must not be overlooked: They trust the laity to be effective in ministry. In 1994, Christ Church embarked on a new path: training lay pastors to lead the ministries of the church. Lay pastors give leadership in three areas: First, they lead Wesley Fellowship Groups, Christ Church's small-group discipleship system. Second, they give leadership in administrative groups, such as finance, trustees, and other similar groups. Third, lay pastors give leadership to action ministries, such as ushers, clothing ministries, prison ministry, choirs. Each group that meets at least once a month must have a lay pastor.

Christ Church has specific requirements for its lay pastors: First, each lay pastor must commit to a daily time of prayer and Scripture reading. Second, each lay pastor must be spiritually focused with intentionality in his or her area of ministry. Third, the lay pastor must fill out a brief form each month so that the church office knows who has joined or left that ministry area. Fourth, lay pastors must attend a monthly training of lay pastors. If a person misses the meeting, then he or she is no longer a lay pastor. If that person comes back and renews his or her commitment, he or she can become a lay pastor again.[8]

In the twentieth-century structure, the congregation came to worship to see what the pastor was doing. Did he or she preach a good sermon? Did the pastor attend all the meetings, visit the sick, and attend to all the needs of the church's members? In the twenty-first-century structure, the pastor comes to worship to experience and reflect on what the congregation has been doing. Did they feed the poor, visit the sick, pray for healing, and attend to the needs of the congregation and the community?

I often hear the following question when I explain this model of leadership: "Where in the model does the ordained pastor fit?" The answer is that his or her work is "in the arrows." (See "5.8. Structure for the Twenty-First-Century Ministry System," on page 73.) The ordained clergy's responsibility, along with the leadership core, is to make sure the flow of ministry is happening throughout the congregation.

A New Look at an Old Practice

Some may wonder where this model for structuring and doing ministry outlined above comes from. A look at the birth of the Christian church in Chapters 1 and 2 of Acts provides a hint. Before Pentecost, the disciples and the women who followed Jesus devoted themselves to prayer and discernment: "All these were constantly devoting themselves to prayer, together with certain women, including Mary the mother of Jesus, as well as his brothers" (Acts 1:14). Before the Holy Spirit came upon these believers on the Day of Pentecost, they devoted themselves to prayer and discernment. For the church today it means that before empowerment and vision, come devotion and spiritual discipline.

According to Acts 2:42, new believers practiced specific spiritual disciplines: "They devoted themselves to the apostles' teaching and fellowship, to the breaking of bread and the prayers." It was out of these acts of faith that ministry followed. As a result, they received new believers into their midst on a daily basis, because these new converts saw how much the believers practiced what they talked about.

As we follow the story of the church in The Acts of the Apostles, we find that the problem was not getting new followers; the problem was what to do with them after they arrived. For the early church, vision, prayer, and call came *before* structure and ministry were put in place.

Returning to the Core

The challenge for the church today is that congregations find themselves living somewhere between the structural and leadership models of the twentieth-century church and the twenty-first-century church. Most believers grew up in the Modern structure; most clergy have been trained to lead the Modern church; and many members find meaning in serving in positions of leadership in the Modern-church structure. But most would agree that these former ways of doing things are not working anymore and that something has to change.

Paul's prayer for the church in Ephesus is helpful at this point:

> I pray that the God of our Lord Jesus Christ, the Father of glory, may give you a spirit of wisdom and revelation as you come to know him, so that, with the eyes of your heart enlightened, you may know what is the hope to which he has called you, what are the riches of his glorious inheritance among the saints, and what is the immeasurable greatness of his power for us who believe, according to the working of his great power. (Ephesians 1:17-19)

Paul's prayer challenges us to revisit our roots, to ask why we are a church in the first place, and to dig deep in our hearts to hear a fresh call that will propel us into the future. Faith communities that are growing and speaking to people today focus on the call of God to be in ministry in the world. Through the spiritual disciplines of prayer, Bible study, worship, the Lord's Supper, fasting, being accountable to one another, and doing acts of mercy, faith communities are finding the wisdom and the strength to make changes that enable everyone to be freed up for ministry.

This style of responding to God's call is not something new. In the past, when believers gathered for prayer, when they experienced the sacraments, when they sought God first before they acted, when they upheld one another and acknowledged the spiritual gifts of fellow believers, when they lived out of the core values of the Christian faith, they flourished. They shared the gospel with love and conviction, and they created new faith communities that invited others to grow and create together. Congregations become healthy and start to grow when they focus on the core disciplines of the Christian faith. As they grow in faith, a new vision for ministry arises and new life emerges as faith communities minister in the name of Jesus Christ.

Before a congregation launches a worship service, before it starts building, and before it puts in place new structures, it needs to discover the core values of the Christian faith—and live on the basis of these values. Everything the new faith community does is built on this foundation. Vision for ministry arises when a person or a community seeks God first. Rather than trying to manufacture a vision, we allow vision to flow out of practicing the spiritual disciplines of the Christian faith. Ministry brings the vision alive. It comes naturally to those who actively seek and listen to God.

Endnotes

1 From *The Works of John Wesley, Volume 18: Journals and Diaries I (1735–38),* edited by W. Reginald Ward and Richard P. Heitzenrater; pages 124–25. © 1988 Abingdon Press. Used by permission.

2 From *The Book of Discipline of The United Methodist Church—1996;* page 114. Copyright © 1996 by The United Methodist Publishing House. Used by permission.

3 Extract from *George Whitefield's Journals* (Edinburgh: Banner of Truth Trust, 1985), page 38. Banner of Truth Trust, 3 Murrayfield Road, Edinburgh EH12 6EL. Used by permission.

4 From *The Book of Discipline of The United Methodist Church—1996;* ¶62, pages 71–72. Copyright © 1996 by The United Methodist Publishing House. Used by permission. "Christian conferencing (conversation)" is not listed in the General Rules; however, it was basic to the life of the early Methodist meetings, and John Wesley lists it in other plans. "Acts of justice and compassion" is interpreted, not quoted, from the *Discipline.*

5 See *Baby Boomer Spirituality: Ten Essential Values of a Generation,* by Craig Kennet Miller (Nashville: Discipleship Resources, 1992), page 66.

6 For a detailed explanation of the Postmodern Generation, see *Postmoderns: The Beliefs, Hopes, and Fears of Young Americans (1965-1981),* by Craig Kennet Miller (Nashville: Discipleship Resources, 1996).

7 Adapted from *Waking to God's Dream: Spiritual Leadership and Church Renewal,* by Dick Wills; page 56. © 1999 Abingdon Press. Used by permission.

8 See *Waking to God's Dream: Spiritual Leadership and Church Renewal,* by Dick Wills (Nashville: Abingdon Press, 1999), pages 60–63.

Chapter Six

LEADING A HEALTHY CORE GROUP

Monastery of Saint Joseph of Avila, Spain, 1577

What the devil is hereby aiming after is no small thing: the cooling of the charity and love the Sisters have for one another. This would cause serious harm. Let us understand, my daughters, that true perfection consists in love of God and neighbor; the more perfectly we keep these two commandments, the more perfect we will be. All that is in our rule and constitutions serves for nothing else than to be a means toward keeping these commandments with greater perfection.

Teresa of Avila[1]

Throughout the church there is an ongoing debate about the nature of the church and of the conflict between ordained clergy and laity in local congregations. Much of this comes as a result of the vast changes that are shaking up the culture as a whole and, in turn, the lives of those who make up the body of Christ. As was stated in the previous chapter, local congregations are grappling with what it means to be in ministry in the twenty-first century while at the same time operating out of a twentieth-century model.

As a result, leading a congregation is becoming more and more difficult. Ordained ministers are operating in the world of the twentieth century, but are being challenged to change by books such as this one. Trained to lead the twentieth-century church, they wonder whether they will ever be able to make the changes necessary to lead their church in a different direction.

On the other hand, lay members of the congregation are tired of ordained ministers coming to their church and trying the latest fad, making them feel as if what they have been doing has been worthless. Or they are longing for something new, but the ordained minister is content to do it the same old way.

Additionally, clergy and laity alike are increasingly stressed by life in the fast lane. On top of the stresses at work and school, families find themselves on the front line of the cultural wars. Divorce and separation are just as likely to happen in clergy and church families as in the culture at large. Stresses over the roles of men and women, finances, and the use of time stretch our capacity to love and care for one another. In the wake of the school shootings that have torn at the fabric of society, parents are fearfully seeking a safe place for their children.

These pressures and issues do not suddenly disappear when people show up at church. In many cases, conflicts in the church are fueled by the disappointments and struggles of living in the twenty-first century.

Rather than focusing on the heart of what is going on, we tend to focus on the symptoms. We argue over styles of worship, over the kinds of music we should play, over finding the right curriculum that mirrors our values, and how to reach the "new people" who have moved into the community. But what is overlooked in these debates is a far deeper issue: How do we treat one another, and what is in our hearts?

My contention at this point is that what is at the heart of many of the conflicts and issues that divide is an inability to trust and to love one another. Before a congregation can grow spiritually and numerically, before it can effectively start new faith communities, it has to perform open-heart surgery. The congregation has to look at its reason for being and at how its leadership is living out the Christian faith.

The Core Group

In every congregation there is a core group, which is made up of the leaders of the congregation who invest themselves in the life of the congregation. They may lead small groups and Bible studies, serve on committees and teams, or actively participate in the worship life of the congregation. They may sing in the choir, usher, or serve as liturgists. They may lead mission projects to help the poor, teach Sunday school, or serve as youth leaders. These people are seriously committed to the life of the church and find meaning and purpose in what they do.

The way this core group works together, prays together, and encourages one another affects the whole life of the church. Its vision of what the church is supposed to be like, its hopes for the future, and the values of the core group are seen throughout the life of the church.

Ideally, ordained ministers and church staff are seen as part of this core group. Like the laity, they have a stake in the future of the congregation. They, too, bring values, beliefs, and spiritual gifts to the table.

When a new person becomes the pastor of an existing church, the first leadership job for the pastor is to create a healthy core group. A new-church planter faces the same task. Why? Because the relationships between people in the core group are key to the future ministry of the congregation. As Matthew 7:16-20 says:

> You will know them by their fruits. Are grapes gathered from thorns, or figs from thistles? In the same way, every good tree bears good fruit, but the bad tree bears bad fruit. A good tree cannot bear bad fruit, nor can a bad tree bear good fruit. Every tree that does not bear good fruit is cut down and thrown into the fire. Thus you will know them by their fruits.

This Scripture passage brings home a point that is often missed in the establishment of new faith communities (either in a new church or in an existing congregation): If the tree is rotten, it cannot produce good fruit; if it is healthy, it produces good fruit in abundance. What is at the heart of the congregation affects the whole ministry and witness of the congregation. To say it another way, if the members of the congregation's core group hate one another, the congregation is going nowhere. If the core group members love one another, the future can be built on a solid foundation.

Healthy Relationships—
The Heart of a Healthy Core Group

What exactly do we mean by a *healthy* core group? Galatians 5:19-26 spells it out pretty clearly:

> Now the works of the flesh are obvious: fornication, impurity, licentiousness, idolatry, sorcery, enmities, strife, jealousy, anger, quarrels, dissensions, factions, envy, drunkenness, carousing, and things like these. I am warning you, as I warned you before: those who do such things will not inherit the kingdom of God.

81

By contrast, the fruit of the Spirit is love, joy, peace, patience, kindness, generosity, faithfulness, gentleness, and self-control. There is
no law against such things. And those who belong to Christ Jesus
have crucified the flesh with its passions and desires. If we live by
the Spirit, let us also be guided by the Spirit. Let us not become
conceited, competing against one another, envying one another.

Paul makes a point of saying to the Galatian church: "I am warn-
ing you, as I warned you before." This phrase is instructive, for it
shows us that Christians and congregations are just as prone to works
of the flesh as is anyone else. But this fact does not let congregations
off the hook; instead, these kinds of actions are not to be tolerated.
The list of the works of the flesh is instructive for us to consider.

The first three—fornication, impurity, licentiousness—have to do
with sexual activity outside the bounds of Christian morality. How
many churches have been torn apart by affairs of pastors and leaders
in the congregation? How many people have been hurt because of
instances of sexual harassment or an act of sexual abuse of a child
or youth? While much focus has been on the clergy, it is equally
harmful when members of the congregation—especially those in
positions of authority—engage in such activities. We all could tell
sordid stories of congregations whose leadership core has been
shredded by acts of sexual immorality.

The next two works of the flesh—idolatry and sorcery—are
related to religious practices. Since church leaders are on the forefront of living a spiritual life, these two works of the flesh can easily
creep into their lives.

The next eight—enmities, strife, jealousy, anger, quarrels, dissen-
sions, factions, envy—affect the nature of our relationships. Recently,
I visited a worship service in a local church. Coming in a little late, I
sat down toward the back of the sanctuary. As I participated in the
service, I became increasingly upset with a group of members of the
congregation who were sitting behind me. Whenever the pastor
spoke, they made comments about the quality of the pastor's voice,
clothes, and message. This group didn't even bother to whisper; their
comments could be heard clearly three or four pews ahead of them. I
do not know what possessed them to do such a thing, but obviously
this was a congregation in great discord.

Throughout the Christian church we find ourselves in deep conflict
over a wide variety of issues. Many of these are critical issues having
to do with the future of the church; but when we allow such issues to
destroy the nature of our relationships to God and to one another, we
endanger who we are called to be: disciples of Jesus Christ.

As I travel across the church, many times I feel the deep pain of people in ministry—both laity and clergy—who find themselves in the midst of hellish battles over the future of their congregations. In most instances, what lies at the heart of the matter is the inability to treat one another as fellow followers of Jesus Christ. Years of unresolved conflict and dissension—even hatred—swallow up the best of intentions and kill the ministry of many Christians whose only real desire is to serve in the name of Christ.

The last two works of the flesh on Paul's list—drunkenness and carousing—contain an addition: "and things like these." These works of the flesh have to do with addictive behaviors that cut at the root of what it means to follow Christ. Rather than following Christ, believers caught in addictive behaviors find themselves following another master, whether it is alcohol, drugs, gambling, sex, or food. All these tempt people to escape from unresolved pain in their lives.

You may wonder why I bother to bring up Paul's discussion of the works of the flesh. In many ways, this passage of Scripture becomes a litmus test for what it means to live as a healthy core group. And the passage does not end here, for it offers an alternative: the fruit of the Spirit.

The listing of fruit of the Spirit is not just for individuals; this description also gives us a picture of what our relationships with one another are meant to be. The fruit of the Spirit tells us how we should interact with and treat one another. As one grows in spiritual maturity, his or her life is to be infused with the fruit of the spirit. The fruit of the Spirit, like a cluster of grapes, is made up of a number of characteristics that, when seen together, give us an image of the attributes of a follower of Jesus Christ: "The fruit of the Spirit is love, joy, peace, patience, kindness, generosity, faithfulness, and gentleness, and self-control" (Galatians 5:22–23).

When John Wesley talked about "going on to perfection," he was pointing to a Christian lifestyle whose attributes were marked by the fruit of the Spirit. These attributes are not given to us in an instant; rather, we grow into them as we mature in faith. These attributes are at the heart of healthy relationships, the kind of relationships that encourage the believer and congregation alike to grow in faith and action.

How does a core group and, in turn, a whole congregation move in this direction toward healthy relationships? Once again, Paul offers insightful advice:

> If we live by the Spirit, let us also be guided by the Spirit. Let us not become conceited, competing against one another, envying one another. My friends, if anyone is detected in a transgression, you who have received the Spirit should restore such a one in a spirit of gentleness. Take care that you yourselves are not tempted. Bear one another's burdens, and in this way you will fulfill the law of Christ.... So then, whenever we have an opportunity, let us work for the good of all, and especially for those of the family of faith. (Galatians 5:25–6:2, 10)

It is fascinating to see how focused these words of wisdom are on the way Christians are to treat one another. Paul's emphasis on the inward life of the congregation should cause us to ask why the way we treat one another is so important. For Paul, it is important because our witness to those outside of the faith depends on the nature of our relationships to one another as people of faith.

One of the keys to being effective in ministry is that what you say and do is real. *Real* is seen in the way people treat one another: Do they love one another? Do they treat one another with respect? Do they pray for one another? Do they pray every day? Do they seek God's will in all they do? Do they help those who are in need? How do they treat one another when conflicts arise? Does adversity divide them, or does it cause them to seek God's will as they work together for the common good?

The goal of tending to relationships is not to avoid conflict. In fact, conflict is a natural part of human relationships. When we work together, we will have differences of opinion; we will see things from different perspectives, sometimes even opposite points of view. But that is how it is supposed to be. Sometimes the dissenter in the group has the answer or the right solution that everyone else has been unable to see.

The question for the core group of a local church is not how to avoid conflict; the question is how to treat one another when conflict does happen. Adversity brings out the true nature of our relationships with God and with others. Through adversity and change, the congregation is challenged to grow in understanding, faith, and trust.

Basic Building Blocks of the Christian Life

In 1577, Teresa of Avila was asked to write down her understanding of prayer. At age sixty-two, Teresa (who had given her life to Christ in her teenage years) was seen as someone who had reached Christian perfection. In her writing she likens the soul to a castle filled with rooms. As one enters each room, one grows in understanding of the deep mysteries of God. She says: "Insofar as I can understand, the gate of entry to this castle is prayer and reflection."[2]

For Teresa, prayer is at the heart of the Christian life—not prayer filled with empty words, but prayer and reflection that draw the believer deeper into the life of faith. Teresa's words challenge us to look at what we might consider the basics of the Christian life: prayer, Bible study, holding one another accountable, worship, and acts of mercy.

A leader starting a new church comes to it with the expectation that new participants in the community of faith must be taught these basics. Leaders do not expect new believers to act like believers until they have been shown the basic practices of the Christian life. Leaders do not assume that all people already know the basics of the Christian lifestyle.

As a result, leaders of new churches prepare materials to teach new believers these basic Christian practices. They teach people how to pray; they help people discover their spiritual gifts; they show people how to have a daily devotion; they put people in places of outreach where they can begin to see God's work in the lives of other people; they show people how to worship from the heart. Even more important, the leaders live these basic practices themselves—or the whole thing just doesn't ring true.

Unfortunately, many existing churches operate on the assumption that their members already know the basics of the Christian life. But if prayer and Bible study have not been part of a congregation's life in years, on what basis does a congregation make that assumption?

It may seem simplistic and obvious that the way to develop a healthy core group—and, as a result, a healthy congregation—is by learning the basics of the Christian life and living it out. However, many leaders skip this step to get on with the "real" business of the church, such as creating new worship services or new ministries to the poor. But they skip this step at their own peril. Without a solid core group, the whole church can fall apart at the first sign of disappointment or conflict.

The Roles of Christian Leadership

Priscilla and Aquila as Models of Leadership

A close look at the start of the ministry in Ephesus shows us that Priscilla, Aquila, and Paul put much time and effort into creating a healthy core group. First Corinthians 16:19 points to the key role of Priscilla and Aquila in the building of the new faith community in Ephesus. Writing from Ephesus to the church in Corinth, Paul says:

"The churches of Asia send greetings. Aquila and Prisca, together with the church in their house, greet you warmly in the Lord." The New Testament church did not build buildings for worship and for meetings; instead, they met in households. Some households (those of the more affluent) could hold from fifty to one hundred people. Priscilla and Aquila were able to offer their household as a place for this emerging congregation to meet.

Going through the text of Acts 18 and 19, we can identify different types of people in Ephesus who were gathered into the core group of the new congregation. This process of forming a core group did not happen instantly. Approximately nine months to a year was spent gathering the core group for this new faith community.

After Paul had left for Jerusalem, a man named Apollos appeared in the synagogue (Acts 18:24-28). Apollos was from Alexandria, and although he was well versed in the Jewish Scriptures (Old Testament) and had been instructed in the Way of the Lord, Priscilla and Aquila noticed that he lacked some knowledge about the Way of God: He didn't know about the baptism of Jesus. It is important to realize that many strains of Christianity were prevalent in the regions surrounding the Mediterranean Sea. Twenty years had passed since the resurrection of Jesus, and word of this miraculous event had spread. Along with those who followed Jesus were those who had been disciples of John the Baptist, some of whom we will meet in a moment.

Priscilla and Aquila represented the strain of Christianity that could be traced directly to the Jerusalem church and to the apostles. After Apollos had finished speaking, Priscilla and Aquila pulled him aside and told him privately about the baptism of Jesus. Notice that they did not challenge him as he was speaking; nor did they seek to embarrass him before others. For them, leadership was more than just proving they were right. They saw themselves as ones who were to instruct and guide fellow believers about the ways of God. They were living out of the fruit of the Spirit.

This leadership style was not unique to them. In 1 Timothy 1:3-4, we find another leader of the church in Ephesus who was to follow the ministry of Paul, Priscilla, and Aquila—namely, Timothy. Writing to Timothy somewhere between A.D. 62 to 66, Paul says:

> I urge you, as I did when I was on my way to Macedonia, to remain in Ephesus so that you may instruct certain people not to teach any different doctrine, and not to occupy themselves with myths and endless genealogies that promote speculations rather than the divine training that is known by faith.

Teaching People Christian Doctrine

The example set by the leaders of a faith community shape the core values and the life of the core group of the congregation. In turn, these values of the core group give shape to the role of leadership in the local congregation. Throughout First and Second Timothy, Paul gives guidance and direction regarding the role of leadership in the congregation in Ephesus. First and foremost was the importance of teaching and instructing people in right doctrine.

William J. Abraham, in *Waking From Doctrinal Amnesia: The Healing of Doctrine in The United Methodist Church*, makes a convincing argument as to why it is important for churches to have doctrinal standards.

> Why do churches, including the early Methodist Church and its sister bodies, develop standards of doctrine? There are clearly a host of reasons, and we can readily identify why early Methodists did so in the eighteenth and nineteenth centuries. Broadly the reasons are human, social, pastoral, and evangelistic. Human beings, both corporately and individually, are very naturally driven to articulate those convictions which form and shape their lives. At a deep level intellectually, we are agents who need to put the insights and ideas that really matter to us into relatively comprehensive systems of teaching. Socially, we are forced by circumstances to explain our corporate identity to friends and foe. One way to do this is to draw up doctrinal summaries which explain who we are and what we believe. Pastorally, doctrinal schemes provide road maps for sorting out who we are, how our lives are made whole, and how we are to live in the world. In this respect they provide a pivotal role in preaching, pastoral care, and spiritual direction. Finally, for evangelism doctrinal proposals spell out the content of the gospel and the rudiments of basic teaching which are passed on to a new generation of Christian children and converts. Thus evangelism depends for its execution on convictions about creation, human nature, sin, salvation, and the like.[3]

In the context of the city of Ephesus in the first century, knowing what you believed and why was critical. The city was filled with various belief systems and religious rites common to cities in the Roman world. Not only were Priscilla and Aquila contending with itinerant speakers who spoke of Jesus Christ from a different understanding of his mission and ministry, but they also found themselves in a city well-known for magic, occult practices, and mystery religions. Alongside these was the worship of the various gods of the Greek and Roman religions, with their temples and religious practices. Moreover, the worship of Artemis was a major source of income for the city.

Right doctrine was one of the central issues for the early church because Christianity was a unique alternative to the religions and cultural practices of the time. Beliefs about God, Jesus Christ, the Holy Spirit, sin, grace, the sacraments, and Scripture were key to Christians' ability to invite others to join the Way. The whole New Testament can be seen as a series of writings penned for the purpose of helping others know the beliefs and practices of the Christian faith.

Christian churches in the twenty-first century face many of the same issues. Each congregation needs to define its beliefs, doctrines, and faith statements because in the age of the Internet, one cannot assume that people know who you are or what you believe just because you say you are a church. Are you the Church of Scientology or the Church of Religious Science? Are you connected with white supremacy or the New Age movement? Almost any group can say it is a church. In a world of alternatives, what does it mean to be a Christian church? How do people know who you are?

Proclaiming a Transforming Word

The second leadership role is proclaiming the word from God. Paul challenged and instructed Timothy to proclaim the gospel: "I solemnly urge you: proclaim the message; be persistent whether the time is favorable or unfavorable; convince, rebuke, and encourage, with the utmost patience in teaching" (2 Timothy 4:1-2).

One aspect of proclamation is the articulation of God's call to the congregation. Convincing, rebuking, encouraging, and teaching are all part of the proclaimer's tools to help shape the lifestyle and the witness of the congregation. Another way to say it is that through the preaching ministry the pastor has the unique role of casting the vision of what that congregation is to become as it follows Jesus Christ.

However, proclaiming God's call is not done in a vacuum. The proclaimer must listen to the needs of the congregation, to the needs of the wider community in which the congregation is located, and to God as he or she shares the vision. The word is the proclaimed word of the community of faith that challenges preachers and listeners alike to live a new life in obedience to God.

One of the tests for leadership in the congregation is whether the leadership core attends worship. Often, the ones most upset with the direction the church is going are those who are not attending worship. Because the worship service and the preaching is the central place where the vision of the church is articulated, people can easily lose track of where the congregation is heading when they do not attend.

One local church decided to meet this issue head on. Their administrative board worked to determine criteria for leadership in the church. They came up with specific practices that leaders did as part of church life. One of their criteria was faithful attendance at worship. Working together, they determined that one of the requirements for serving in leadership positions was the commitment to attend worship forty weeks out of the fifty-two weeks of the year. They felt that this would go a long way toward developing a core group that was on the same page. Along with faithful worship, the leadership also committed to daily prayer for the church, for other members of the core group, and for the pastor.

Equipping Believers for Ministry

A third key leadership role is equipping believers for ministry. Second Timothy 3:16 says: "All scripture is inspired by God and is useful for teaching, for reproof, for correction, and for training in righteousness, so that everyone who belongs to God may be proficient, equipped for every good work."

Ephesians 4:11-13 carries the same theme:

> The gifts he gave were that some would be apostles, some prophets, some evangelists, some pastors and teachers, to equip the saints for the work of ministry, for building up the body of Christ, until all of us come to the unity of the faith and of the knowledge of the Son of God, to maturity, to the measure of the full stature of Christ.

The critical emphasis in both these passages is that leadership equips believers to be in ministry. The job of the leader, or the leadership core group, is not to do the ministry on behalf of others. Instead, the goal of the core group is to infuse people with the passion to be in ministry in the world and to give them the tools they need to be successful.

Two of the tools for ministry are articulated here. One of these is helping believers know the Scripture. The second is helping believers know their spiritual gifts. Combined, these tools enable believers to know why they are doing what they are doing and to have the power to fulfill the ministry to which they are called.

As a congregation works to create a healthy core group, knowing the Scriptures and the spiritual gifts of the group members is a key place for the core leadership to start. By knowing Scripture and discerning their spiritual gifts, these leaders begin to get a bigger picture of what this combined ministry can become.

It was with an understanding of their role as leaders who equip others for ministry that Priscilla and Aquila approached Apollos after hearing him speak (Acts 18:24-28). Not only did they explain God's Word to Apollos, but they also recognized in him a gift for teaching and preaching (Acts 18:27-28).

Shortly afterward, Apollos departed for Achaia. You may wonder how the Ephesian congregation could let such a leader go. If he was so gifted, shouldn't they have done everything they could to keep him in Ephesus? Wasn't he more important to the emerging congregation in Ephesus than to the one in Corinth?

By encouraging Apollos in his call, by letting him go to do the ministry that God called him to do, Pricilla and Aquila were giving a powerful message to the new community of faith in Ephesus: The work is not about us; it is not self-serving. This is God's work. Our goal is not simply to meet the needs of the people in our new faith community in Ephesus; our goal is to serve God and to send believers out into the world to share the gospel of Jesus Christ.

The Role of the Pastor

One of the key issues related to developing a healthy core group is the role of the pastor. Two basic pictures of pastoral leadership exist out of which a local church can operate. The first is that of the pastor as *cleric*. The role of the cleric is to do all the ministry of the church on behalf of the congregation. The pastor visits the sick, attends all the meetings, preaches, teaches, administers the sacraments, ministers to the poor, evangelizes the lost, and so forth. In this model, the congregation's role is to provide the resources needed for the pastor to do his or her job. They pay the salary, provide for housing, and provide a space where the ministry can take place. In some sense, they see the pastor as being hired to minister to their personal needs and to represent the church in the community.

The second model is much different. In this picture, the role of the pastor is that of *visionary leader*. In this role, the pastor's job is not to do the ministry for the congregation, but rather to challenge believers to be in ministry. The pastor calls people to be in ministry and equips them to do the ministry. The visionary leader focuses on three important aspects of the congregation's life: developing a healthy core group, articulating the core values of the congregation, and articulating a vision for the future.

Pastoral Leadership in an Existing Congregation

Typically, when a pastor first arrives at an existing church, the members of the church view him or her as a cleric. They see the pastor as one who has been hired to do the ministry in the local congregation. The pastor is then judged on the basis of his or her ability to do the job and care for the members' needs.

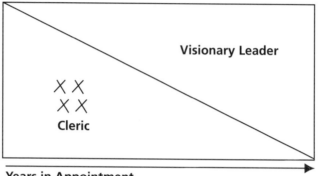

6.1. Pastoral Leadership in an Existing Congregation

I remember one experience I had with this. After preaching at the first service of an existing church to which I was appointed, one of the leading members of the congregation came up to me and said: "I think this is going to work." I took this as a positive statement, but the comment also articulated where I was in the pecking order of leadership. When a pastor enters a new situation, he or she is the new kid on the block and has to earn leadership. The new pastor is not automatically seen as the visionary leader.

About four years into the life of a new pastorate, the congregation often finds itself in conflict. This conflict, which is part of a natural process and happens in virtually every congregation, may come sooner; but it will happen, one way or another.

What is the nature of the conflict? It has to do with the role of the pastor. Typically, after a pastor has been in a church for about three years, a new group of people will have joined the congregation. These people do not see the pastor as a cleric; they view the pastor as the visionary leader. This is especially true of new Christians who have made their faith commitment during the ministry of this pastor.

When the number of newcomers reaches a "critical mass," members who were part of the church before this pastor came to serve the church will begin to wonder where they themselves fit into the leadership of the congregation. Often, splits will take place over those who support the pastor's viewpoint and those who do not. The conflict is about who is the leader and who will lead the congregation in the future.

6.2. Conflict Over the Role of Pastor

In the United Methodist system, when this kind of conflict occurs, pastors often are moved to another church. When this happens over and over again, the congregation develops layers of unresolved conflict over leadership and the direction of the church. The process starts over every time a new pastor is appointed; and when conflict arises, it is time to move. When the pastor and the existing leaders of the congregation have been unable to create a healthy core group, the congregation seeks a change because this is the only way they have learned to operate in the past. Instead of seeing conflict as a natural part of the growing process in the congregation and learning to deal with conflicts, the leaders of the church and the pastor bail out before the conflict is resolved.

Visionary Leadership Prepares for the Future

Rob Weber, founding pastor at Grace Community United Methodist Church in Shreveport, Louisiana, saw one of his primary roles as that of casting the vision of what the community of faith is to become. After four years of meeting in a high school, the new church was preparing to move to its brand-new building. Rob knew that one of the tendencies of new congregations is to feel as if they have finally made it when they have their own facility. To counter this tendency, Rob prepared his congregation for the move by preaching a series of sermons on the Book of Exodus and the challenge of moving to the Promised Land. Rob said that like the Promised Land, the new building was not for those who were currently in the congregation; the new building was for the whole community. The new building would be another tool the congregation would have to use to call people to become followers of Jesus Christ, now and in the future.

Rob's example points to the importance of visionary leadership for a congregation. Rather than dwelling in the past or staying put in the present, visionary leadership anticipates the spiritual needs of the congregation as it grows and matures. Without visionary leadership, a church can stagnate or become content with its success. Rather than saying they had arrived, Grace Community came to realize that the new building presented them with a new opportunity to reach new people.

Blocks to Visionary Leadership

Invariably, some congregations will have leaders who never get onboard with visionary leadership. One of these leaders might be a pastor who loves the role of cleric and is reluctant to let others be in ministry. He or she enjoys the one-on-one contact of ministry and sees the pastor's role as being the primary caretaker of the congregation. But this approach has consequences.

First, members of the congregation become disenfranchised ministers. They are never taught or given permission to discover their call. By holding onto the entire ministry of the congregation, the pastor keeps others from discovering and using their own gifts for ministry.

Second, this approach limits the growth of the congregation. One person can do only so much. Pastors who see themselves as the only ones who can do ministry limit the ability of the congregation to grow, to reach out, and to incorporate new members.

Another group that may never buy into visionary leadership are long-time members who have been disappointed by previous experiences with pastors. They may find it hard to trust another pastor. Or there may be long-term members who have so much at stake in the current way of doing things that they do not wish to share leadership or to give up power.

In the case of pastors who love the role of cleric, they either learn to give away ministry so that others can be in ministry or they move to another congregation every four years or so. Or, conversely, they spend years trying to be the congregation's caretaker, while their congregation loses members and never grows.

The case of long-term members is harder to decipher. One hurdle congregations often face is whether or not the leadership core will allow a small group of dissenters to stop the growth of the congregation. Growth is not just numerical; it also has to do with spiritual growth, maturing in faith, and being guided by the Holy Spirit. When the congregation's core group is healthy, growth in numbers and spiritual growth come naturally. When people block this growth, the leaders have to make tough decisions as to whether this group is going to be allowed to kill the direction of the congregation. Congregations who give in to the dissenters over and over will find themselves dead in the water. They will never grow until a healthy leadership core is developed and allowed to move forward in response to God's call.

When vision for ministry grows out of the practice of prayer, Bible study, worship, holding one another accountable, and doing acts of mercy, all believers in the congregation see themselves as ministers of the gospel. When the pastor moves into the role of visionary leader and articulates the call of God to this particular congregation in this place and time, the congregation is able to respond and move forward.

This process takes time because it is dependent on believers developing healthy relationships with one another. It is no coincidence that churches that are growing have pastors who have been there long enough to create a healthy core group whose members trust one another, actively seek God's will in all they do, and equip believers for ministry.

I like to joke that The United Methodist Church needs to change the itinerant system. The pastor should stay in place while the congregation moves. In fact, in most of our communities, this would be a truer picture of what is going on. When both the pastor and key leaders of the church move over and over, vision is hard to articulate and maintain. But United Methodists are not alone in this. Rick Warren, senior pastor of Saddleback Valley Community Church in Orange County, California, and one of the most effective pastoral leaders of our time, makes this point in his book *The Purpose-Driven Church: Growth Without Compromising Your Message and Mission*:

> Healthy, large churches are led by pastors who have been there a long time.... A long pastorate does not guarantee a church will grow, but changing pastors every few years guarantees a church won't grow....

Churches that rotate pastors every few years will never experience consistent growth. I believe this is one reason for the decline of some denominations. By intentionally limiting the tenure of pastors in a local congregation, they create "lame duck" ministers. Few people want to follow a leader who isn't going to be around a year from now. The pastor may want to start all sorts of new projects, but the members will be reticent because they will be the ones having to live with the consequences long after the pastor has been moved to another church.[4]

A Healthy Core Group

One of the critical problems in many congregations is that during the first three to four years of a pastorate, the congregation never develops a healthy core group—made up of the pastor, some long-time members of the church, and some of the new members who have joined during the years the pastor has been there. One of the vital keys to moving through any conflict is for the leadership of the congregation to intentionally focus on developing healthy relationships by focusing on the spiritual disciplines and living out of the fruit of the Spirit.

A congregation that has developed a healthy core group is able to move the congregation through a time of conflict over pastoral leadership. After the crisis is over, the most successful years of ministry for both the pastor and the congregation can take place.

6.3. A Healthy Core Group Leads Into the Future

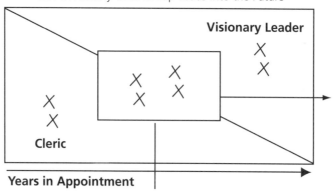

You may ask, how do we do this? A couple of things can move you toward developing this leadership core that can guide the congregation through the times of conflict. First, tell others about the information in this chapter. Help people see that conflict over these issues is a natural part of the development of the leadership core. Second, help the leadership core determine what spiritual practices they are going to commit to as leaders of the congregation: How often will they pray? What does faithful worship attendance look like? Do they read the Bible? How often? In other words, have the leadership look at Wesley's means of grace and ask what this means for your life together. (See "5.2. Wesley's Means of Grace," on page 61.) Third, hold one another accountable. At the beginning of each leadership meeting, ask the group about their spiritual lives. Fourth, begin each committee meeting, task group, or team session with a time of prayer, Bible study, and reflection. Ten to fifteen minutes of spiritual enrichment at the beginning of a meeting is not wasted time; it is time that focuses people on why they are there in the first place.

Most importantly, the pastor also must agree to the same commitments the leadership core makes and must be willing to be held accountable to the same criteria as the rest of the leadership core. When the pastor is vulnerable and willing to confess his or her struggles and successes, it brings a refreshing change to the dynamic of leadership. Leaders are real people in the service of God.

Developing Core Groups to Start New Faith Communities

Core groups are not just for the top leadership of a congregation. One of the critical steps in creating new faith communities (with a worship experience connected to a discipleship system, in an existing congregation or in a new church) is developing a core group that leads that new ministry. When a new worship service fails, often it is because the church staff of the church tried to launch the service without developing a strong core group. The core group are the people who will support and lead this new ministry.

When Curt Sylvester came to Saint Joseph United Methodist Church in Fort Wayne, Indiana, in 1983, he found a worshiping congregation of slightly more than two hundred people. Today Saint Joseph offers six worship experiences on the weekend and three during the week, with an average attendance of more than nine hundred. One of the keys to the success of this church is that it takes the development of the core group seriously. Before any new ministry is launched (including a new worship experience), a core group is gathered to practice the spiritual disciplines, to hold one another accountable, and to prepare for the new ministry.

As the leadership of Saint Joseph prepared to launch a new worship experience called Great Adventure in a strip mall, a core group of about thirty people spent two years together. Along with prayer and Bible study, core-group members were taught how to lead small groups, how to mentor new Christians, and how to do visitation. Five of the lay members worked with one of the ordained pastors to learn how to preach and lead worship, so that they could be developed to become the preaching/worship team that leads the worship. On Wednesday nights the core group met to practice the upcoming worship experience, including drama, contemporary music, and proclamation. After two years the church launched the new worship experience publicly. It now has more than 160 people in worship on Sundays and offers a focused "believer experience" on Wednesdays. The goal is not to get people to come to the church at the Saint Joseph site, but to develop and sustain Great Adventure on its own site.

Saint Joseph United Methodist Church has launched many new ministries in the same way, beginning with a core group to give leadership. The significance of this last point is not to be missed. Saint Joseph is not just starting new worship experiences. They are starting new *faith communities* that include a discipleship system consisting of small groups and of worship. At the heart of these new faith communities is a core group of people whose ministry is to create and sustain this ministry of the church.

Characteristics of the Church Planter

When a pastor or church planter starts a brand-new church, a different dynamic takes place. From the beginning, this person is seen as the visionary leader of the congregation. As a core group is developed, it will buy into the vision of this new ministry. If the pastor or church planter operates out of the cleric's role, the congregation that develops will be focused on having the pastor take care of all their needs, and their future growth will be limited. If the pastor or church planter takes on the mantle of visionary leader, he or she will equip the core group for ministry, will teach them the basics of the Christian faith, will guide them in developing spiritual disciplines, and will free them to discover their own ministry.

While some may think it would be great to create a new church from scratch without having to overcome bad histories, nothing could be further from the truth. The reality is that creating a new church is an awesome responsibility that is not to be taken lightly.

Suddenly, your spiritual life and your relationship to God is before the world. The only thing you have to offer is your conviction that God is calling you to start a new ministry in this community. The only thing that attracts people to the new ministry is a compelling vision. When you start new, you do not have a building, a program, or a community service to offer. Because of these things, some key characteristics are needed for new-church planters.

First, a new-church planter must be grounded in his or her spiritual life. No amount of charisma or self-confidence can take the place of a life of prayer. Daily prayer, daily study of the Bible, faithful attendance at worship (as a worshiper, not as the leader of worship), and times of spiritual retreat and reflection are all important for spiritual vitality. The new-church start is not about you; it is about creating a new faith community that will be obedient to God and will bring others into a new relationship with Jesus Christ.

Second, a new-church planter must be willing to be held accountable. Starting new churches is not a job for lone rangers. One of the first tasks is to develop a network with other people who are not part of this new ministry to be encouragers and prayer partners for the church planter. Finding a mentor who has been through the process of starting a new church can be an important part of the puzzle.

Third, a new-church planter must have a stable family life. Many new-church starts fail because the church planter did not take into account the stress this new venture would place on his or her family. The whole family must be committed to the task in order for it to work.

Fourth, a new-church planter must be flexible and ready to try new things. Like a baseball player, his or her success is not judged on getting it right every time. If you can hit the ball three out of ten times, you are doing well. The key is being able to learn from mistakes and being willing to seek out the information you need when you need it to take the next steps in the development of the congregation. Church planters who are lifelong learners attract people who want to learn.

Fifth, a new-church planter must have a passion to reach and teach those who do not know Jesus Christ. Many new-church starts have failed because they were built on a cause, rather than on helping people know Jesus Christ. New churches make it or break it depending on how well they are able to develop a discipleship system that moves people from being seekers to being believers to being disciples of Jesus Christ. While a limited number of people will join a cause, an unlimited number of people can be transformed through a relationship with Jesus Christ.

"First Things" as the Pattern for the Future

Acts 18:19-28 tells us that Paul had left Priscilla and Aquila in Ephesus while he went to Jerusalem. While one of the tasks of Priscilla and Aquila was to learn about the region, the task of finding like-minded people who might want to be part of this new faith community was even more important. Having already led house churches in Rome and Corinth, they had the spiritual gifts for this type of ministry. Through their work as tentmakers, they were able to provide for their physical needs as they developed the ministry. To debate whether Priscilla and Aquila were clergy or laity would miss the point. They were disciples of Jesus Christ, whose gifts enabled them to help Paul lay the foundation for what in the future would be known as the church in Ephesus.

Before launching the public ministry, which is the phase when everyone in the community is invited to join in public worship, Priscilla and Aquila concentrated on gathering together a healthy core group. This group, who sought to live out a Christian lifestyle as a witness to others of the saving grace of Jesus Christ, became the foundation on which the new faith community was built.

Often the biggest mistake leaders of new congregations make is moving too quickly to public worship. If worship is started without an adequate core group or discipleship system in place, the new congregation constantly has to try to catch up. Instead of creating a faith community, such a congregation has created a worship experience without a way for people to grow in faith and practice. When leaders spend their time thinking about how to offer a worship experience every week, the time that could have been spent on developing the discipleship system and core group is gone.

When Paul returned to Ephesus, he spoke to two groups. First, he encountered a group of disciples of John the Baptist and told them:

> "John baptized with the baptism of repentance, telling the people to believe in the one who was to come after him, that is, in Jesus." On hearing this, they were baptized in the name of the Lord Jesus. When Paul had laid his hands on them, the Holy Spirit came upon them, and they spoke in tongues and prophesied—altogether there were about twelve of them. (Acts 19:4-7)

This group became part of the core group of the new congregation. Next, Paul entered the synagogue and for three months spoke out boldly and argued persuasively about the kingdom of God. In this instance, he was articulating the vision of what it means to be a follower of Jesus Christ. After the three-month period, he took those who had caught the vision and started the new work.

Together Priscilla, Aquila, and Paul gathered a core group before launching the public ministry. They focused on living out of the fruit of the Spirit, taught the basic beliefs and practices of the Christian faith, and equipped and released people to be in ministry. Together they laid the foundation on which this future work was to be built. They took their time, focused on the essentials, and gathered a healthy core group that would birth this new community of faith.

Healthy Leadership Builds Healthy Churches

In both new and existing churches, leadership makes or breaks the future of the local congregation. Leadership that focuses first on developing a healthy core group best positions the congregation for change and for moving into the future. This process may take from one to four years, depending on the situation in which the church finds itself. This process of developing the core is not for the impatient. It takes time, prayer, confidence, and dependence on the Holy Spirit to move beyond issues related to buildings and programs to focus on forming healthy Christian relationships that nourish the soul and create a strong foundation for spiritual and numerical growth.

Critical to the process is a leader who is willing to say, "I need to grow in love and compassion." Leaders who do not have all the answers but have a desire to work with others to discover the answers are ones who create an atmosphere where healthy relationships can develop. Healthy leaders create healthy core groups and, in turn, healthy congregations.

Endnotes

1 From *Teresa of Avila: The Interior Castle,* translated by Kieran Kavanaugh, O.C.D., and Otilio Rodriguez, O.C.D.; page 47. © 1979 Washington Province of Discalced Carmelites, Inc. Used by permission of Paulist Press.

2 From *Teresa of Avila: The Interior Castle,* translated by Kieran Kavanaugh, O.C.D., and Otilio Rodriguez, O.C.D.; page 38. © 1979 Washington Province of Discalced Carmelites, Inc. Used by permission of Paulist Press.

3 From *Waking From Doctrinal Amnesia: The Healing of Doctrine in The United Methodist Church,* by William J. Abraham; pages 37–38. © 1995 Abingdon Press. Used by permission.

4 From *The Purpose-Driven Church: Growth Without Compromising Your Message and Mission,* by Rick Warren; page 31. Copyright © 1995 by Rick Warren. Used by permission of Zondervan Publishing House.

Chapter Seven

SHAPING THE DISCIPLESHIP SYSTEM

Milan, 1498

Leonardo's *Last Supper* captures, with stunning psychic force, the moment that Christ proclaims, "One of you shall betray me." Christ sits alone, resigned and serene, at the center of the table as the disciples explode in turmoil around him. Yet in a geometrically perfect composition, the disciples counterbalanced—left and right, high and lower—in four groups of three, Leonardo brings the uniqueness of each soul to life. Christ's tranquillity, conveyed through Leonardo's seamless sense of order and perspective, contrasts with the surrounding human emotion and chaos to yield a moment of transcendence unparalleled in the history of art.[1]

One morning I received a frantic call from a pastor of a new church. Using one of the popular techniques for gathering a large crowd for a first worship service, the pastor and his core group had called more than fifteen thousand people in their community. Over the course of three months, they had sent out a series of mailings to a number of people who had responded positively to the idea of a new church in the area. On their opening Sunday, more than two hundred people showed up. But there was a small problem. He asked me, "*Now* what do I do?"

In the excitement of launching the first public worship experience, the pastor and the core group had not paid attention to a vital step that sometimes is easy to bypass: They had failed to think through the need for and the place of a discipleship system in the new congregation. They had neglected to ask themselves: *What do we hope will happen in the lives of people as they become part of our faith community?*

Have you ever had this experience? A new family with small children visits your worship service. You can't help but hear the man's wonderful tenor voice. The children mind themselves and make little noise during the service. Afterward, you turn around and say, "You have a wonderful voice. You're a tenor, aren't you? We really could use you in the choir. Is this your wife? Your children seem to be so well mannered. We really could use another pair of hands in the nursery."

Many times those of us in the church see visitors as the answer to our latest problem or need. Rather than think of what we can offer newcomers as they seek God, we think of the needs of the institution—the congregation.

I was talking with a group of people in a church when one of them remarked: "The day I joined the church they put me on the evangelism committee. They thought I knew how to reach people for Christ, since I was new. I didn't have a clue. Why do they do that to people?"

We do this for many reasons. The most likely reason is that this is what was done to us. Because the local church has institutional needs—keeping the lights on, staffing volunteer positions, keeping programs going—new people are seen as the life blood that keeps things going. When we joined the church, we more than likely found ourselves fed into a system whose goal was to turn us into good committee members or workers in church programs. In most congregations, little thought is given to the idea that there might be more to church that taking on the hallmarks of membership.

Why Come Back?

A long-term member of a church once told me the following story. She was walking down the sidewalk to the front entrance of the church when she overheard two young men having a conversation about the church. One of them said, "I don't get it. Don't they already know the story about Jesus? Why do they keep going back?"

It's a question that is well worth asking. Leonardo da Vinci is considered by many to be one of the greatest geniuses in history. One of his greatest accomplishments is the painting *Last Supper,* which is seen by many art historians as one of the finest of all time. In this painting, Leonardo was able to bring to life the struggle of following Jesus.

Through this masterpiece, Leonardo challenges each of us to look at our motives and reasons for following Jesus. What are you really all about? What experiences have shaped your understanding of God? What do you expect or hope for others as they seek God? Are you a different person because of your Christian faith? Are you still growing in faith? Do you feel that God is done with you, or is God preparing you for the future? Do you have a reason to keep going back?

The Spiritual Journey

When a person gives her or his life to Christ, is that the end or the beginning of the journey with God? Your answer will say a lot about how you view the Christian life. If you say that it is the end of a person's search for God, you are assuming that the goal of the Christian life is to become a believer. Once you are a believer, your name is written in the book of life and what you do for the rest of your life is icing on the cake. Sure, you may stumble here and there; but because you professed your belief in Jesus Christ, you are guaranteed a place in heaven.

This perspective tends to be the perspective of church leaders who view the ultimate goal of church life as getting members. Once a person becomes a member of the church, that person is in—one step away from heaven. From then on, all he or she has to do to be set for eternity is perform faithful service and give financially.

But think about the following for a moment. Say someone who comes to your church is impressed by the Christian witness of the congregation. Somehow God stirs life in the person's soul. Finally, this person renounces her old life and gives her life to Jesus Christ. In a dramatic act of faith, she is baptized and received into the community of faith. For this person, baptism and reception into the fellowship of the church is a life-changing experience of the grace of God.

But soon afterward the pastor calls her into his office and offers her a position on the administrative board. After a couple years, she gets invited to usher at the Sunday morning worship service. Is serving on the administrative board and ushering really the ultimate goal of the Christian life? Is this really all that the church has to offer?

The second perspective says that once a person gives his or her life to Christ, it marks only the beginning of the Christian journey. While conversion starts when someone says yes to God's call, it is not a one-time event; rather, conversion is a lifelong process. The rest of his or her life is to be spent growing in faith, witnessing to others and serving them in Christ's name, and learning more about the Christian way.

With this second perspective, the role of the church is different. Rather than being the holding pen for believers waiting to get to heaven, it becomes the training ground for Christian witness and ministry to the whole world.

Ways of Thinking in the Twenty-First Century

Living in the twenty-first century brings with it three ways of thinking that affect the way people relate to one another and get things done. The first way of thinking is the emphasis on *lifelong learning*. In the past, parents would pass on a trade to their children. A farmer would show his son or daughter how to farm, with the expectation that he or she would follow in the father's footsteps. Today, that is seldom true. In fact, many people under age thirty expect to have from five to seven careers. As a result, they can never afford to stop learning. For example, as information technology increases the ability to research and develop new products and treatments for illnesses, doctors have to keep up with what is going on or else they will become out of date quickly.

This attitude toward learning translates to spirituality as well. Rather than adopting one set of beliefs that stays unchanged throughout a lifetime, people want to grow and learn as they advance in spiritual maturity. Paul addressed this same issue when he wrote in Ephesians 4:14-15: "We must no longer be children, tossed to and fro and blown about by every wind of doctrine, by people's trickery, by their craftiness in deceitful scheming. But speaking the truth in love, we must grow up in every way into him who is the head, into Christ." Spiritual maturity and growth is the expected result of the Christian life.

The second way of thinking is *systems thinking*. Research in many different areas has revealed the interconnectedness of life. Rather than each of us doing his or her own thing, we know that our actions affect others. Systems thinking forces us to think of our work as a system in which relationships and tasks are interrelated and mutually dependent. While not using systems language, Paul was thinking systemically when he compared the life and work of the church with that of a body: "[Christians] must grow up...into Christ, from whom the whole body, joined and knit together by every ligament with which it is equipped, as each part is working properly, promotes the body's growth in building itself up in love" (Ephesians 4:15-16).

When the congregation pays attention to the whole system—to all the relationships and structures that make up the body of Christ in that place—they are able to address needs effectively as they arise.

The pastoral leadership in one church found that they had a problem with weddings. The two pastors realized that they were taking turns doing premarital counseling and weddings just about every week;

therefore, they were getting tired of having their Saturdays taken up with weddings. They were meeting the needs of the couples who were getting married, but they were getting burned out in the process.

When the pastors began thinking about the congregation's wedding process as a system, they realized that the system was not yielding the results they wanted. Therefore, they decided to redesign the system. The pastors looked over the church's calendar well in advance of the weddings to determine a reasonable number of days for each pastor to do weddings. The new system worked like this: Each quarter, couples who were planning to get married were invited to be part of a small group that would go through premarital planning and preparation together. Leaders from the congregation were recruited to help lead the sessions. Afterward, the wedding coordinator met with each couple to go over the specifics of the wedding. One of the pastors met once with the couple before the wedding so that they could get to know one another better and prepare for the wedding. Couples were also strongly encouraged to attend worship so that they could get to know the pastors and the congregation better. Suddenly, the pastors felt they had some control over their time.

Couples were invited to come back together after the weddings to form a small group that would focus on making it through the first year of marriage. Since the first year of marriage sets the pattern for the relationship and is therefore the most critical time, having the support of the small group proved to be of great benefit to the couples.

The important point of this example for our purposes is that by designing a discipleship system for weddings, the congregation was able to connect the preparation for the wedding with ongoing support and discipleship after the wedding. The message from the congregation to the couples was clear: The congregation was not going to abandon the couple after the wedding ceremony; they were going to provide a network of support as the newlyweds moved into married life.

The third way of thinking is *teams*. Rather than having employees work on projects in isolation, with each doing his or her own thing, many companies have found great success in putting people together in teams. The difference between teams and committees is that once a meeting is over, everyone on a team takes responsibility for carrying out the decisions the team has made. Instead of having one person to blame if things go wrong, the whole team takes ownership of both the successes and the challenges of the project. In this way, they learn together and improve what they are doing.

The Primary Task

The way a faith community applies these concepts—lifelong learning, systems thinking, and teams—to its own life is by focusing on its primary task: making disciples of Jesus Christ. The primary task is not a set of individual tasks, each to be performed at different times by different groups or individuals. Instead, the primary task is an integrated process. Therefore, everything that happens in the life of the congregation reflects this fourfold process: (1) reaching and receiving new people into the faith community; (2) creating settings where people can connect to God; (3) nurturing and strengthening faith through the practice of the spiritual disciplines; and (4) sending people out into the world to be in ministry as disciples of Jesus Christ. The primary task, then, runs through the whole life of the congregation as a process of spiritual development.

7.1. The Primary Task

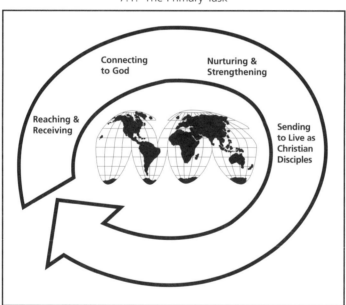

In the past, the four components of the primary task often operated independently of one another. For example, a congregation would have an evangelism committee for reaching and receiving new people, a worship committee for connecting people to God, an education committee for nurturing people in the faith, and a mission committee for sending people into the world. When functioning as a system, however, the four components of the primary task are intermeshed in a way that creates a flow of spiritual development within the total life of the congregation. Everything that happens in the congregation incorporates these four aspects and thus brings the primary task to life.

Viewing the primary task as a *discipleship system* means that every area of the church's life is responsible for reaching and receiving new people into the faith community. This is not just the job of the pastor or of one committee. Each aspect of the life of the faith community—whether it be small groups, worship, or Christian education—has to build into its ministry the task of reaching new people and receiving them in the name of Christ.

Let's take the worship experience and the small group as an example of how the primary task may function as a system of discipleship. Worship that is visitor-friendly helps reach and receive new people into the faith community. The worship experience is a setting where people are connected to God. As people participate in a worship experience, they are nurtured and strengthened in their faith. As they pray together, hear the reading of the Scripture, and take Holy Communion, they are availing themselves of the means of grace. They therefore grow in faith and practice. During worship they are equipped to go out into the world to be in ministry as disciples of Jesus Christ. The primary task, then, runs through the whole worship experience, with the goal of making Christian disciples.

The same is true of a small group. When people are invited to participate in a small group, they are being reached and received. The small group itself is a setting where people are connected to God. Through the practice of prayer, Bible study, and accountability to one another, participants are nurtured and strengthened in their faith. However, the process does not stop there. As individuals go into the world, they know that they are supported by their small group through prayer and encouragement to live a life of service and witness.

The Discipleship System

One of the vital tasks during the first six months of a new church's development is to form and articulate what the discipleship system will look like. Likewise, one of the critical steps for turning around an existing congregation is to evaluate and improve its current discipleship system. The way to approach the development of a discipleship system in either case—a new church or an existing congregation—is to ask: "What does our faith community need to offer to help a person reach spiritual maturity in the first three years of being a part of the faith community?"

Spiritual maturity encompasses such things as a person's prayer life, his or her understanding and knowledge of the Bible and the basic beliefs of the Christian faith, faithful participation in worship, awareness of his or her spiritual gifts, active participation in a small group, growth in the fruit of the Spirit, service in the community, and discovery of the ministry to which God has called him or her. Each congregation—new or existing—needs to wrestle with what spiritual maturity looks like. Two questions can help congregations:

■ What are the essential beliefs of the Christian faith?
■ What spiritual disciplines do we commit to as active members of this faith community?

The Discipleship System as a Process

Congregations that have set up discipleship systems successfully do so in a way that fits the people group they are serving. One model for structuring the discipleship system might be to offer a series of learning opportunities, progressing along a scale of complexity. For example, a class titled "Christianity 101" would focus on introducing learners to basic Christian beliefs, while the more-advanced "Christianity 201" class would deal with prayer and the spiritual disciplines. The third-level class, "Christianity 301," would guide participants in discovering their spiritual gifts. The fourth-level class, "Christianity 401," would focus on helping people discover the particular ministry to which God is calling them. Together, these classes function as a system of discipleship, in that they help people learn the core values and mission of the congregation, develop their practice of the spiritual disciplines, discover their gifts for ministry, and capture and articulate their vision for ministry.

The classes listed above would be core classes, which would be taught in the congregation on a regular basis. All who came to the local church would be encouraged to go through this discipleship process, with the goal of equipping themselves to discover their own gifts and be in ministry in the world.

Another model for creating a discipleship system might be more organic. In this model, the church would offer a series of experiences in which people encounter God—alone or through ministry to others—followed by small-group sessions in which the individuals can reflect on these experiences. One experience might be a silent retreat in which people would use the silent time to focus on their relationship with God. Afterward, the retreat participants would gather in small groups to focus on prayer and the spiritual disciplines. The purpose of this small group would be to build on the retreat experience by helping participants go deeper into the spiritual life of prayer.

Another experience in this model might be a mission trip in which participants minister to poor and disenfranchised people. To follow up on the experience, participants would gather in a small group to discuss what it means to be in ministry to people beyond the congregation. Yet another experience might be to stage a family camp that focuses on God's gifts to the body of Christ. Instruction at the camp would focus on discovering one's spiritual gifts and on the relationship between spiritual gifts and spiritual growth. After the camp is over, participants would form small groups for continued instruction, exploration of spiritual gifts, and learning how to use their spiritual gifts for the building up of the body of Christ.

In this second model, the focus is on building into the life of the congregation a series of experiences, teaching opportunities, and settings designed to lead to spiritual maturity. This model differs from the first in that each individual picks which experience to participate in; also, the individual determines his or her readiness for an experience. However, like the first model, the second model also functions as a process of discipling.

Preaching as Part of the Discipleship Process

The preaching ministry can echo this discipleship process as well. For example, the preacher may follow the first model by tailoring the week's message for a 101 level, thus talking about the core values of the Christian faith. The next week the sermon could be on a 401 level, focusing on God's call to each Christian to be in ministry in the world. *Level* does not imply a hierarchy of inferior and superior knowledge; rather, the word refers to the people's level of spiritual development and readiness. Over the course of a year, the preacher keeps a balance in terms of the level of spiritual development he or she addresses in worship. Remember that in this model, preaching is relational and focuses on equipping the believers for ministry.

The goal of the discipleship system is to engage people in a process of spiritual growth and development that moves them into ministry beyond the congregation. The process of discipling described here is different from assimilation. The goal of assimilation is to help "them" become like "us." In a discipling process, the goal is to help believers discover their ministry and to reach out to the people group they are uniquely gifted to reach. Such ministry is not a solo affair. A discipleship system is designed so that core groups are developed who together can create new ministries for the people groups the core groups are called to serve.

The Strategy of the Early Methodists

The discipleship system of the early Methodists was focused on key aspects that help us think through our own discipleship process: First, they lived a practical Christianity that spoke in the language of the people. This practicality was most clearly seen in the use of music, which was indigenous to the people the Methodists were trying to reach. Rather than the high-church music used in the cathedrals, new music was developed that was modeled after tunes sung in the local pubs. Early Methodism's practical Christianity focused on the whole person. Education, health, politics, and the wider culture all played a part in the lives of those who were in the faith community. Thus the faith community needed to work in the wider world to create ministry and strategies that helped the whole person. What made Methodists different was their desire to integrate their newfound experience with God into the way they lived their daily life. The new way of living affected all aspects of life.

Second, Methodists were taught spiritual disciplines that helped them grow in faith and practice. By practicing the means of grace, believers grew in faith and moved toward perfection in love.

Third, people were held accountable in small-group settings for their Christian lives and witness. Meeting together regularly with fellow believers to inquire after the state of one's soul was a vital part of spiritual growth and development.

Fourth, believers were expected to do acts of mercy, to be in ministry to the poor and the disenfranchised. Faith was something to be given away, not kept to oneself.

Fifth, all the baptized were called and challenged to be in ministry. Ministry was not just the prerogative of the church cleric; everyone who believed in Jesus Christ had a ministry. And one expressed one's ministry through using one's spiritual gifts so that the body of Christ might be built up and equipped for ministry.

7.2. The Strategy of the Early Methodists

- A practical Christianity that speaks in the language of the people
- Personal holiness
- Accountability in small groups
- Acts of mercy
- Ministry of the baptized

Designing a Discipleship System

Every church I know of that is growing spiritually and numerically is able to articulate an image of its discipleship system. For some congregations the image might be that of a baseball diamond; for others, it might be a funnel or a well. Whatever the image might be, the leaders in growing congregations are able to share with newcomers the process of discipleship.

Use Worksheets 5–8 in the Appendix (pages 181–84) to help develop a healthy leadership core and a discipleship system in your congregation. These graphics are meant to help a leadership team work through a process of evaluating the congregation's current ministry system and of developing a discipleship system that will be effective. For new-church starts, the graphics show how to develop a new core group that will launch the public ministry in the future.

Endnotes

1 From *How to Think Like Leonardo da Vinci: Seven Steps to Genius Every Day,* by Michael J. Gelb; pages 27–29. Copyright © 1998 by Michael J. Gelb. Used by permission of Dell Publishing, a division of Random House, Inc.

Chapter Eight

SETTINGS
FOR VITAL
MINISTRY

**April 1997,
Milpitas, California,
in the heart of the
Silicon Valley**

After nine months of developing a core group and marketing to its community, Genesis United Methodist Church is launched, with more than 320 people in its first public worship service. Participants are invited to attend seminars and small groups to deepen their walk with God.

What function does a local church have that makes it unique in the spiritual life of the community in which it resides? A church cannot make someone believe in God. It cannot force people to attend worship. Nor can the church make people relate to God in some fashion. So what does the church actually do?

The church creates settings where people can connect to God. What do I mean by settings? In Matthew 18:20, Jesus says: "For where two or three are gathered in my name, I am there among them." The church is where people gather in the name of Jesus Christ.

Christians gather together in two different types of settings: First, there are the informal settings that happen in daily life. When a family says grace before a meal, they are gathering in the name of Jesus Christ. At school or at work, an informal setting is created when two or three gather in Christ's name for prayer, encouragement, or instruction. Virtually anywhere a Christian goes and meets with another Christian, a setting is created where Jesus

Christ is present with them. The leaders of a local church cannot create these informal settings, but they can encourage the believers to create them. Those settings are outside the control of the local church.

Second, there are the formal group settings that are specifically created to invite people to gather in the name of Jesus Christ. It is in these settings that the church comes into play. What the congregation can do is provide and create the formal group settings where people can experience the means of grace, gather for instruction, encourage one another in their Christian walk, and come together in worship.

Group Settings for Ministry

As the new faith community in Ephesus developed its ministry, it found itself operating out of two group settings: First, they met in house churches (such as that of Priscilla and Aquila). It was in these house churches that the process of discipleship took place. In these settings of small groups, believers focused on studying the Scripture, learned how to pray, and discovered their gifts for ministry.

The second group setting, which was much larger, was where proclamation took place. It was in the synagogue and then in the lecture hall that the Word of the Lord was proclaimed. In the public setting, the focus was on telling people about the life and ministry of Jesus Christ. The goal was to let all people, Jew and Greek alike, know about the life-changing power of faith in Jesus Christ.

This focus of ministry—equipping believers and public proclamation—was present in the early church from the beginning. Acts 2:41-42 gives us a picture of how the new believers lived out their faith:

> So those who welcomed [Peter's] message were baptized, and that day about three thousand persons were added. They devoted themselves to the apostles' teaching and fellowship, to the breaking of bread and the prayers.

After baptism, believers were encouraged to live a Christian lifestyle. Their life together was lived out in four aspects: First, they devoted themselves to the apostles' teaching. (For us these teachings are part of the Scriptures.) The teachings of the apostles were based on the teachings of Jesus. Just as Jesus taught them, so the leaders in the fledgling church taught the new believers. The Scriptures contained the stories of faith that gave the lives of the early Christians meaning and hope and served as the bedrock of the early Christians' understanding of God. The basic purpose of the apostles' teaching was to equip the believers for service to others.

Second, the believers gathered together in fellowship to share their dreams, to encourage one another, and to live together as a people of the Way. In their living together they became witnesses to others. The fellowship they shared was a reflection of the fellowship the disciples experienced with Jesus. For three years, the Twelve had lived with Jesus in a community of faith. The newly formed Christian fellowship was in relationship with Christ—the risen Christ—and existed for the building up of the believers.

Third, the early Christians remembered, in the breaking of the bread, Jesus' sacrifice on their behalf. Eating the meal together was closely linked to the many meals the disciples shared with Jesus, especially the Last Supper. Today, too, Christians experience the healing and wholeness offered through faith in Jesus Christ when they eat together at the meal called Holy Communion.

Fourth, the prayers were the air that the believers breathed. Through prayer, the early Christians deepened their connection to God and to one another. Through prayer, vision and a passion for ministry unfolded as these believers sought to follow God's will for them as a community of faith. Because of Jesus' example and instruction about prayer, they were compelled to be a people of prayer.

When balanced, these four elements of the Christian life build and create a community of faith that is able to move forward and outward into the world in order to be a witness for Jesus Christ. Through the prayers, people are given vision for their lives and for ministry in the world. Through the apostles' teaching (Scripture), they are equipped for ministry. The fellowship forms the home base into which others are invited and out of which believers are sent to transform the world. In the breaking of the bread, the community of faith witnesses to others about the saving grace of God found through the crucifixion and resurrection of Jesus Christ.

Acts 2:46-47 completes the picture:

> Day by day, as they spent much time together in the temple, they broke bread at home and ate their food with glad and generous hearts, praising God and having the goodwill of all the people. And day by day the Lord added to their number those who were being saved.

Unlike the mystery religions of the time, and unlike the restrictions found in Judaism, these early Christian settings—equipping believers in small groups and proclaiming the Word in public places—were open to newcomers. In these settings, newcomers heard about the gospel, witnessed the lifestyle of the believers, and were welcomed to be in conversation with believers about the Way.

Having said all this, we should not overlook the source of the growth of the Christian community: God. It was God who gave the growth. Churches cannot manufacture growth; growth results when the Christian community is living in such a way that it is a witness to the saving grace of Jesus Christ. And the best way for the church to demonstrate Christ's saving grace is to provide the settings where Christians can be witnesses as they gather in the name of Jesus Christ.

These two settings—the small groups in house churches and the public worship in the temple—were vital for the early ministry of the church. The small-group setting was where believers were supported and encouraged to grow in their faith. The large-group setting was where public proclamation was made about the claims of the Christian faith.

A Two-Fold Ministry in Three Settings

Today, growing congregations practice in three settings the twin foci of ministry: equipping believers for faithful discipleship and public proclamation of the Word.

8.1. Settings for Congregational Life

SMALL GROUP (5–15)	FELLOWSHIP/ INSTRUCTION (50–80)	CELEBRATIVE WORSHIP (120+)
Practicing spiritual disciplines	Everyone knows your name	Glorifying God
Focused on personal growth	United by single focus	United by worship experience
Diversity found in multiple groups	Homogeneous cultural perspective	Diversity accepted, as there is room for everyone

Setting One: The Small Group

The first setting is the small group. This group has from five to fifteen members and meets regularly to practice the spiritual disciplines, to hold one another accountable, and to focus on personal spiritual growth. A small group typically meets the needs of a particular people group in the church whose members share similar circumstances.

A small group may be united by the level of spiritual maturity; therefore, one may find in a given congregation both a small group for new-member orientation as well as a small group engaged in an in-depth Bible study such as DISCIPLE. One may also find in the same congregation a Covenant Discipleship group for those who want to go deeper in their relationship with God and others.

Small groups may be united by family circumstances, so the congregation may have a singles group, a married-couples group, and a group for single parents.

Alternatively, a small group may be united by a personal issue, such as twelve-step groups for alcoholics or groups convening around issues of substance abuse or how children of alcoholics may cope with their parents' addiction.

Other groups may be generational in orientation, such as youth prayer groups or Bible-study groups for older adults. Some small groups may be focused on outreach into the community; other groups may be task-oriented, such as a worship team, an administrative board, or a choir.

By offering a number of small groups that address different constituencies and needs, a congregation makes room for great diversity in its total life. Rather than having everyone in the church focus on one or two issues, each small group is able to meet the spiritual and social needs of individuals within the framework of a small-group system.

Setting Two: The Fellowship/Instruction Group

The fellowship/instruction group typically has from fifty to eighty members. In this size group, participants more than likely know one another by name. The group tends to be homogeneous, uniting itself around one people group. The people group may be ethnic or generational, or it may be a family group in which relatives of all ages gather together. The group is united by a *single focus*, dealing with the particular life issue or life stage its members deem significant.

A large youth group or a fellowship group that has been meeting together over the course of many years is an example of the fellowship/instruction group. In my home church, the Polaris Group has been meeting together for more than fifty years. It started as a fellowship for young marrieds; today, it is for people who are in their seventies and eighties. In many ways, the members of the group have grown up together. Their unity is unwavering and life-sustaining.

In many congregations, the fellowship/instruction group is the size of the worshiping congregation. Because of its size, the worship experience in such congregations tends to be focused on fellowship and the care of members.

Setting Three: The Celebrative-Worship Group

Celebrative worship, unlike a praise service or a liturgical service, is not tied to a particular format. In celebrative worship, the focus is on the *type of experience* that happens in a large-group setting. When I speak in front of a group of more than 120 people, participants seem to be freer to express emotions, such as laughing at a humorous story or nudging a friend as if to say, "Did you hear that?"

In a group consisting of more than 120 people, individuals can move freely, express themselves, and draw closer to God during a celebrative-worship experience. This group is united not by intimacy with others but by its focus on the worship of God. Because of its size, the celebrative-worship group allows great room for diversity, so that a large range of people in different circumstances or stages of life can find their place as they worship God together.

Understanding Group Dynamics

Groups that are larger or smaller than the three basic groups outlined above experience a different dynamic. When a small group grows larger than fifteen members, it starts to struggle because the intimacy that attracted members in the beginning is no longer present. Groups with between sixteen and forty-nine members struggle with self-identity as they grow—and the bigger they are, the more the dissatisfaction grows. The solution to this problem is to divide the group into two or more small groups, thus allowing a group size in which people can once again experience intimacy, trust, and greater interaction.

Small groups are defined as having from five to fifteen members. But four can be a perfect number for meaningful discussion. No one person can dominate in this size group, and everyone can participate.[1] This four-person setting fosters greater interaction of the participants, and for that reason is sometimes used for breakout groups in the fellowship/instruction model.

Some popular Bible-study models use a combination of the fellowship/instruction setting, the small-group setting, and the four-person setting in one teaching session. The session starts with the leader giving a half-hour lesson on a section of Scripture. Afterward, the group is divided into small groups or four-person groups, where members discuss reflections, pray for one another, and offer mutual support.

When fellowship/instruction groups grow to between 80 and 120 members, another dynamic takes place. As the number in the group increases, participants feel greater levels of discomfort, and the group struggles with its sense of identity. As soon as a participant realizes that he or she is unable to cope with the increased size of the group, he or she begins to struggle to fit into the life of the group. If such a person is not moved into a small-group setting where he or she can experience a new kind of intimacy, the individual may experience a feeling of being lost in the crowd. (See "10. Dynamics of Group Settings and Settings for Ministry Survey," on pages 186–87.)

Dangers of Exclusive Use of Fellowship/Instruction Groups

An understanding of the nature of the three basic group settings outlined above is critical for the future spiritual and numerical growth of a congregation. Churches with fewer than one hundred people in worship typically have everything (worship, fellowship, instruction, prayer support, and the practice of the spiritual disciplines) in the fellowship/instruction setting. In many cases, this setting acts as a natural barrier to growth. When the size of all the groups is the same size as the worship experience in a congregation, newcomers often find it hard to fit in, especially if they don't meet the homogeneous criteria of this size congregation. And the members of the group who have not had any other group experience often resist numerical growth.

Resistance to growth will continue to build until the congregation is able to move people into smaller groups for instruction or socialization. Until the worshiping congregation breaks through the 120-member barrier, they will have a hard time understanding the benefits of being part of both small groups and a larger worship experience.

In addition, a congregation in a fellowship/instruction setting can go only so far in terms of spiritual growth. A group this size is not conducive to the personal sharing, intimate prayer, accountability, and discipleship that happen only in the small-group and four-person settings. As a result, the members' potential for spiritual growth is limited. A number of things can happen. For example, when members of the congregation are invited to be part of small accountability groups, they may say, "But we already know everyone." When they are asked to invite new people to join them for worship, they may respond, "If we have more people in worship, I won't know everyone anymore."

Congregations for which the fellowship/instruction group is the only setting for faith formation are hampered on both ends of the spiritual-growth spectrum, for they are at once too personal and not personal enough. For example, prayers can be neither personal nor visionary. In the small-group setting where mutual trust has been established, people are more likely to request prayer for deeply personal concerns. A member may ask the group to pray for his or her marriage or for a child who is dealing with drugs. In the fellowship/instruction setting, people are quite comfortable praying for "acceptable" concerns, such as for people who are in the hospital or facing serious illness. But if the prayer concerns venture into moral issues or concerns about relationships, group members often become uncomfortable. The unstated rule seems to be: Feel free to tell about your heart surgery, but don't tell us about the fight you had with your spouse last night. In the setting of celebrative worship, prayer focuses on God's vision for the congregation; therefore, going through a detailed list of everyone's illnesses and troubles doesn't work in a group this size. This does not mean that one shouldn't pray for personal problems or issues in celebrative worship; it means only that such issues are better addressed in a different setting.

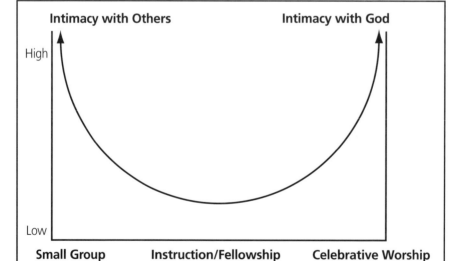

8.2. Intimacy Levels in Group Settings

Growing Congregations Use All Three Settings

Celebrative-Worship Groups Allow Room for Visitors

People in American society don't readily join groups. They like to try things out and then decide if they want to come back. A visitor in a fellowship group of from fifty to eighty people can't hide in the crowd because everyone knows that the person is new. The situation is made worse when visitors are asked to stand and introduce themselves to the congregation. Often, speaking in front of a crowd is one of the greatest fears people have. And yet, visitors who merely want to test the water suddenly find themselves having to convince the crowd that they fit in!

Most people in our culture are more comfortable in large-group settings. Have you ever gone into a movie theatre that seats two hundred and found yourself the only one there? You immediately notice that the sound system is too loud, the air conditioning is blowing too briskly, and the movie is bad. Whether going to a local high-school football game, a movie, or a rock concert, people are used to finding themselves in a crowd.

When new people come to a worship experience, they expect to find themselves in an environment where they can be just one of the crowd. In the celebrative-worship setting, the focus of the experience is on the worship of God. Visitors have room to experience the nature of the worship experience and get a feel for the mood of the congregation without being put on the spot. What is most remarkable is that celebrative worship fosters the individual's intimacy with God.

Fellowship/Instruction Groups Are Perfect for Teaching

The fellowship/instruction group is the ideal setting and size for meeting the expectations of a teaching/learning experience. A group of fifty would be a comfortable size for a seminar on parenting, for it is an informational meeting, a time to learn. Teaching/learning situations have a different set of expectations than larger or smaller groups: No one is expected to sing or to respond in any way other than to take notes and ask questions.

Small Groups Are Ideal for Personal Growth

Many sports teams are the size of small groups. Baseball has nine players on the field; football has eleven. In basketball, you need ten players on the team to practice game situations. People are used to settings this size when the focus is on working together to accomplish a task. The same is true when it comes to practicing the basic

121

elements of the Christian faith. People feel comfortable in a group of from five to fifteen people when the focus is on personal development and growth. Participants feel free to talk about personal issues in a small group, and it is easier to hold small-group members accountable for their actions.

Living Out of the Group Setting in New Churches

The goal for a local church is to operate out of all three group settings. By incorporating all three of the group settings, churches are able to grow spiritually and numerically.

Making use of all three group settings—small-group, fellowship/instruction, and celebrative-worship—is especially critical when starting a new church. The goal at the end of the first year of the new church's life is to have all three group settings operating according to the optimal size and inner dynamics of each group.

When Junius Dotson started Genesis United Methodist Church in Milpitas, California, he intentionally created a congregation that lives out of all three groupings. After spending nine months developing the core group for the congregation and doing the necessary marketing in the community, the leaders launched the first public worship service in April, 1997, with more than 320 people in attendance.

It is important to have as high a number as possible at the first worship experience of a new congregation, for it is typical to see a drop in attendance after the grand opening. Eighteen months later, the worship experience at Genesis United Methodist Church was running at 225 in attendance.

During these first eighteen months, Genesis Church instituted its discipleship system, which consists of fellowship/instruction groups and small groups. Four core seminars are offered to the community. The first seminar, "Exploring Genesis," tells about the core values and mission of the congregation as well as the beliefs of The United Methodist Church. The second seminar, "A Closer Walk With God," focuses on the habits of the spiritual life. The third seminar, "Discovering Your God-Given Potential," helps people explore their spiritual gifts. The fourth seminar, "Becoming Alive in Christ," helps people discover their ministry. Each seminar lasts four hours. After the seminar is over, participants are invited to become active in a small group. Through this process, Genesis Church has developed seventeen small groups.

One of the surprises is that this new African American congregation has attracted a multiethnic audience. In reaching out to the neighborhood, this faith community has found that its ministry speaks to a number of people groups. By providing several different discipleship opportunities in the three group settings, the congregation has put in place a well-developed system for making disciples of Jesus Christ.

Implementing the Groups in Existing Congregations

Creating a new faith community may seem quite daunting for many existing congregations, particularly those with one basic setting—the fellowship/instruction group. The challenge to existing congregations is this: How can the congregation create new settings that allow new people to become part of the faith community? What are the implications for the future of the congregation if it doesn't create such new settings?

Existing congregations can use the charts on pages 185–87 to analyze the dynamics of the congregation as a group. Before thinking about launching a new worship experience, make sure the system is in place to support it. It is best to approach the starting of a new faith community as if one were starting a new church. That means the congregation's leaders focus first on developing a core group and a discipleship system for newcomers. Next, they develop leaders for small groups, as well as start new small groups, with the goal of tying these groups to the new worship experience.

Not all congregations can muster a big enough new worshiping community to use the celebrative-worship model. In such a case, the congregation can offer multiple worship opportunities using the fellowship/instruction model to meet the needs of particular people groups in the community. The rule of thumb is to not stand still. Be creative. Trust God for the leaders and the resources needed to reach out in new ways in the name of Jesus Christ.

Endnotes

1 For a model of how this dynamic can work in a study session, see *Culture Shifts: A Group Bible Study for Postmodern Times,* by Craig Kennet Miller and Lia Icaza-Willetts (Nashville: Discipleship Resources, 1997).

Georgetown, Texas, New Year's Sunday, 2000

When pastor Nancy Woods of Wellspring United Methodist Church proposed that the new church start with two worship experiences on the first Sunday worship was offered, people wondered what that was all about. From the very beginning, Wellspring has offered multiple options in both its small-group ministry and in its worship. More than two years later, on New Year's Sunday, 2000, Wellspring offered three worship experiences with more than 300 people in worship. By starting with multiple options, Wellspring has been able to attract a diverse group of people.

Chapter Nine

LAUNCHING THE PUBLIC MINISTRY

G od's call always demands an action, a response. When God called Moses, it was for a purpose: "So come, I will send you to Pharaoh to bring my people, the Israelites, out of Egypt" (Exodus 3:10). God's call to Abram was the same: "Go from your country and your kindred and your father's house to the land that I will show you...and in you all the families of the earth shall be blessed" (Genesis 12:1-3). When Isaiah heard a voice say, "Whom shall I send, and who will go for us?" he responded by saying, "Here am I; send me!" (Isaiah 6:8). When the angel Gabriel appeared to Mary, she was asked to do something. Mary could have said, "No, I will not give birth to Jesus, the Son of God"; but that was not her answer. She responded to God's call by saying, "Here am I, the servant of the Lord; let it be with me according to your word" (Luke 1:38).

Every new ministry starts with an official launch, the first time the ministry begins. When a new faith

125

community launches its public ministry, a critical stage is reached. After forming the core group and developing the discipleship system, the moment comes when the faith community fulfills the call to proclaim their faith and calls others to receive the saving grace of Jesus Christ. This is true both for existing congregations and for new churches. A new worship service, a redesigned church-school program, the initiation of a new small-group system, the move to a different space for worship, the first time a group goes back into a remodeled space or begins ministry in a new building—all are opportunities to focus on the primary mission of the church: to make disciples of Jesus Christ.

When the believers in Ephesus launched their public ministry, they were clear about its purpose: to proclaim God's Word.

> When some stubbornly refused to believe and spoke evil of the Way before the congregation, [Paul] left them, taking the disciples with him, and argued daily in the lecture hall of Tyrannus. This continued for two years, so that all the residents of Asia, both Jews and Greeks, heard the word of the Lord. (Acts 19:9-10)

The start—the launching—of new ministry provides a faith community with the opportunity to tell its story. The people have to make a case to the community at large as to who they are, what they believe, and what they hope to become in the future.

Preparing to Launch the Public Ministry

After almost a year of identifying people groups, learning about the local culture, and developing a core group and small groups, the faith community in Ephesus was ready for its public ministry. When the faith community moved to the lecture hall of Tyrannus, a new stage in its ministry took place.

Launching the public ministry is a critical stage in the life of any new faith community because the group now moves into an ongoing ministry of public worship and of discipling newcomers. Public worship expands the life of the new faith community by welcoming new people.

When an existing church starts a new worship experience, the process is the same. After preparing, reflecting, gathering data, forming a core group, and developing a discipleship system for the new worship experience, the congregation moves to regular worship on a weekly basis. The pastor and other leaders shift their focus to the preparation of weekly worship and the ongoing discipleship of new believers and those who have been with the faith community from the beginning.

A critical point to remember is that once worship begins on a weekly basis, it is difficult for leaders to create a discipleship system at the same time they are creating worship experiences that truly speak to people's hearts. The process works more smoothly when the discipleship system is created before the first public worship experience. The details can then be changed as needed to meet emerging interests and needs.

What is fascinating about launching the public ministry on the part of the Ephesian believers is that they moved into a public forum where the Ephesian community was used to hearing about new ideas. The lecture hall was perfect for their purpose: spreading the news of Jesus Christ to as wide an audience as possible. So persuasive was the testimony of Paul and the other Christians that by the end of two years, new faith communities were founded throughout the area. In Revelation 2 and 3, the other churches are listed as Smyrna, Pergamum, Thyatira, Sardis, Philadelphia, and Laodicea.

For new-church starts, a fellowship/instruction-size congregation is deadly. The rule of thumb to use when starting new churches is that you do not start the first public worship experience unless you are sure that you will have more than 120 people attending. Many experts would set the bar even higher, to more than two hundred. Although many new churches have started with lower numbers and have grown to the size of a celebrative-worship group, it takes far less time to start with more than 120 in the first place. The number of people attending the first worship service largely determines the future size of the congregation as well as the time it takes to grow larger.

9.1. Attendance at the First Worship Service Is Critical

Worship Attendance in New Church Starts (Total Churches Surveyed: 21)		
Attendance at First Service	Fewer Than 120 After Service Was Started	More Than 120 After Service Was Started
Fewer than 120	63%	37%
More than 120	23%	77%

To put it another way, if you start with fifty to eighty people at your first worship service, it may take you two to three years to move into the celebrative-worship size. History tells us that many congregations are never able to get over that hurdle.

Some might say, "So what? Smaller congregations are good." However, the issue is not size; the issue is spiritual maturity and evangelism. Once a congregation stabilizes at the fellowship/instruction size, it is hard for new people to join. The old rubric that we are a friendly church usually means we already know everyone. As mentioned before, the fellowship/instruction size also keeps people from going deeper in their spiritual walk in small groups and from experiencing the celebrative nature of the celebrative-worship group.

At another level, new-church starts cannot afford to be small. Gone are the days when denominations will buy the land and build a building. Rather, the new congregation will buy the land and build the building as it grows. Unless they are an affluent group of people, the fellowship/instruction group will find it hard to afford to be in business.

It is not unusual for attendance to drop during the second week of a new worship experience, sometimes by as much as fifty percent. But within three years, the worship attendance will have normally returned to the size it was on the day the service was launched. The reason is that those who attended the first worship service and then decided to stay and build the ministry have established in their minds that the attendance at the worship service should be at least the number it was on the day of its public launching. A survey of more than one hundred churches that have started a new worship experience in the last five years proves this point. Seventy-six percent of those churches that started with more than 120 at the first worship maintained that level. Only eighteen percent of those that started with fewer than 120 were able to grow to more than 120. (See "9.2. Growth After the First Worship Service," on page 129.)

What this survey shows is that attendance at the first worship experience sets a number in people's minds that carries over into the future. In each category, the majority of the worship attendance was either the same size or lower than the size of the first service. Even those with more than 120 in the first worship experience found that a couple years later their numbers were the same or lower.

Of those faith communities that started a new worship service with fewer than fifty people in attendance, fifteen percent were no longer meeting, while a further fifty percent continued with worship services that had fewer than fifty in attendance.

9.2. Growth After the First Worship Service

Number of people attending first worship service	Number of churches in survey	% of worship services discontinued	% of worship services continuing with attendance of fewer than 50	% of worship services continuing with attendance of 51–75	% of worship services continuing with attendance of 76–100	% of worship services continuing with attendance of 101–120	% of worship services continuing with attendance of 120+
Fewer than 50	52	15%	50%	17%	6%	2%	10%
51–75	15	14%	0%	46%	14%	6%	20%
76–100	14	7%	0%	21%	29%	0%	43%
101–120	3	0%	0%	33%	33%	0%	33%
120+	25	0%	0%	8%	4%	12%	76%

Based on worship experiences five years old or less. Existing and new church starts reported together. Total Churches Surveyed: 109.

Those who started with fifty-one to seventy-five in attendance were more likely to stay the same size (forty-six percent). Fourteen percent were discontinued, and twenty percent moved to above 120.

Significantly, of those who started with more than 120 in attendance, seventy-six percent were able to maintain that level.

What About a Time Other Than Sunday Morning?

Interestingly, the survey shows that worship experiences that were discontinued were all held at times other than Sunday morning—which brings up an important point: If you are beginning a new worship experience on Saturday or on Sunday evening or during the week, it is vital that you launch the whole enterprise as if it were a brand-new congregation.

When a new worship experience is offered on Sunday morning in an existing church, it is an addition to the schedule of what typically happens. Current members may try it out as a natural part of what they normally do on a Sunday morning. But when a service is at a new day and time, a change is required in the the local congregation's habits. A whole new core group has to be generated to support that worship experience. And remember, if the worship experience is going to become viable in the long run, more than 120 people in attendance at the first service is essential.

The First Public Worship Service
Tells People Who You Are

The first public worship service defines who you are. It sets a picture in the minds of worshipers about the nature of the service and the kind of spiritual experience that is being offered. The first public worship service lets the community see who will be included in your new faith community. The larger the number of people in the first worship service, the more room there is for diversity in the wider congregation. Let me be clear: Diversity refers to more than having a variety of racial-ethnic groups present in the service. Diversity also has to do with such things as the worshiper's family situation, income, job, generation, homeland, and spiritual maturity.

When Nancy Woods, pastor of Wellspring United Methodist Church in Georgetown, Texas, started the church, she intentionally developed a congregation that would be able to minister to a diverse community. After spending nine months gathering people in small groups, Pastor Woods announced the launching of the public worship.

Instead of one worship experience, they offered a traditional one and a more contemporary one. Because two worship services were offered on the first day of public worship, people knew immediately that this new faith community was not operating out of a one-size-fits-all mentality. Through the development of a small-group network and through advertising, the total attendance at both worship experiences was 285. From the beginning, this new church was a place that offered multiple options, both in its small-group ministry and in its worship.

When to Start a New Worship Service

One of the battles new churches face is dealing with the pressure to launch the first worship experience before they are ready. Part of the reason for the pressure lies in the fact that many people equate faithful membership with being in worship. Thus, for them, the first goal is for the new faith community to get the worship experience going, because until that has been done, these people feel that there is no "real" church.

But experience shows that this is the worst reason to start a new worship experience. If a strong core group and a discipleship system is not in place to support the worship service, it will be tough for the new faith community to sustain the service. A new church whose first worship service has only forty or fifty people in attendance often finds itself in a survival mentality from the start and rarely grows to the size of a celebrative-worship group.

If membership size in the congregation becomes a measure of its faithfulness, chances are that participation in a small group will not be viewed as a high priority. In the early church, public worship was only one part of the picture; people also met in small-group settings. A similar dynamic happened in the early Methodist movement. Public proclamation moved people into small-group settings, where heart-to-heart discussion could take place about the nature of each individual's soul. Put differently, at the end of the twelve to eighteen months of its existence, a new church needs to have in place a discipleship system and a celebrative-worship service (or services) that invites people to be disciples of Jesus Christ.

When existing congregations are contemplating starting a new worship experience, they often face the pressure of launching the service prematurely. But as in the case of a new-church start, existing congregations should consider establishing a new faith community that includes a discipleship system for those who attend the worship experience.

More Than One Way to Get There

Many different types of new-church starts exist. Much of the difference has to do with the spiritual gifts and the vision of the church planter and the community in which the congregation is started. Listed below are some types of new-church starts.

Small-Group-Centered Start

The small-group-centered start is developed by establishing a core group and moving them into small accountability groups until eight to twelve groups are established. After the small-group system is in place, public worship is offered for the first time. Typically, 120 or more will attend because of the excitement generated by the members of the small groups.

The North Alabama Annual Conference of The United Methodist Church has started seventeen churches using this model. Before a new church is launched, the church planter starts twelve new small groups, with twelve people in each group. These groups guarantee that at the first worship experience at least 144 adults with their children and youth will be in attendance. By starting with the small-group system first, the congregation has a ready-made discipleship system to which new people can be invited to participate.

When a new faith community is started with small groups, a public worship may not start until nine to eighteen months after the new-church planter begins his or her work. While at first glance it may appear to be a slow process at the beginning, after two years the new church is well on its way with a strong discipleship system and a celebrative-worship service in place.

Worship-Centered Start

The worship-centered start focuses on developing a core group, who will develop and resource a worship experience that will draw people to the new-church start. The small-group discipleship system is put into place under the guidance of the core group after the launch of the new worship service. Through advertising and word of mouth, people are invited to the new-church start.

Some new-church starts have been giving a preview of the worship experience after the core groups have been established. They offer the new worship experience on the first Sunday of the month and then move people into small groups the next three Sundays. They then offer the preview again and repeat the process until they are at the point of offering the worship experience every week.

The worship-centered model requires a successful marketing and advertising campaign for the launch of the worship experience. Some congregations use phone marketing; others use direct mail. The danger of the worship-centered model is that if the marketing does not click, the worship experience will get off to a slow start.

Community-Based Start

Community-based ministry starts with sensitivity to the needs of a given people group and attempts to meet these needs. In this case, the pastor and the core group may offer English as a second language (ESL) courses for new immigrants, start a job-training program for youth and adults, or offer parenting classes for single parents. In the churches I visited in Cambodia, one of the strategies has been to put in a well for fresh water and a fishpond. In the process of meeting the needs, people are gathered together and invited to participate in small groups for spiritual development. A public worship experience is launched when the faith community is ready.

Parenting-Church Start

Another type of new-church start is the parenting-church start. In this model, an existing church uses its resources to launch a brand-new congregation. This was the method used by the church in Ephesus in the establishment of new churches in nearby cities and towns.

One way to plan a parenting-church start is to have the new-church planter appointed as an associate pastor of an existing congregation. The new-church planter will have the specific task of creating and equipping a core group for a new congregation that will be started in a nearby area. The new-church planter, along with the new core group, begins small-group ministry in the area where the new church is to be launched. After a year, the new church is started with the new core group and the small-group ministry in place.

A parenting-church start is especially effective when the existing church is ten years old or less. A new church that sees part of its mission to be the planting of new churches is one that will grow the church in many different ways.

Geoffrey Kagoro, District Superintendent of the Harare West District UMC in Zimbabwe, established twenty-five new faith communities in the first half of 1999 by challenging the existing churches in the district to support the establishment of new congregations. The process was defined: After an evangelist was sent into a new area, nearby churches took turns sending worship teams to lead an open-air, overnight revival worship experience in the new area. These worship experiences took place on the weekends for about two months. During that time, the evangelist and members of the worship teams went door to door inviting people to the worship experience. After two months, a seven-day crusade was held in the area, and the new church was established. The key to this method is that existing churches caught the vision of starting new congregations.[1]

The above list of models for establishing new churches is not an exhaustive one. Much depends on the creativity of the leaders and the needs of the community. In the Appendix you will find a guideline for the first year (pages 168–73) that contains a community survey, which has been successful for ascertaining community needs, and information about resources that are available for new-church starts.

Implications for Existing Congregations

For existing congregations, the challenges and opportunities in creating new faith communities are much the same as for a new-church start. The fact is, congregations that offer only one worship option severely limit their potential for offering ministry to people in the community. In order to meet the many and varied needs of people, congregations need to offer multiple worship options. In other words, an existing congregation can apply to their own situation the following lessons that have been learned about starting new faith communities:

■ First, identify the people group for which the experience is being started.

■ Second, develop a core group whose task is to prepare the congregation and itself for reaching out to new people with this worship experience.

■ Third, identify and shape the discipleship process for people who will be part of this new worship experience. Do not forgot to plan for the children. Such things as church school and nursery care are just as important for this new service as they are for the current worship experiences you offer.

■ Fourth, remember that the size and nature of the worship experience will be determined largely by the number of people who participate the first time the worship service is held. The first worship service will affect who will come in the future, the potential for future growth, and the ongoing purpose of the worship service.

■ Fifth, ask what options you need to offer to believers and potential believers that will extend to them the full spectrum of the experience of God's grace.

Nothing says a church that offers only one worship setting is ineffective or not viable. But the issue I want to push is that as long as a congregation has only one worship option, it limits its potential to offer ministry to both a greater diversity of people and to a wider audience of people in the community.

A congregation that wants to offer celebrative worship as an option will find it difficult to do so if it starts with fifty people or fewer. A congregation's chances for success are better when it takes time to develop small-group or fellowship/instruction-group settings in preparation for launching the celebrative-worship experience. When new worship experiences fail, it is often because the congregation's leaders have not done the hard work of preparation and because the congregation lacks a strong core group to undergird the new worship experience.

Different Ways to Think of Options

If a congregation has one worship experience that is successful, it can repeat the worship experience at a different time, rather than creating a new format. This becomes a new option for those who want to be involved in this church. The Church of the Resurrection in Kansas City, pastored by Adam Hamilton, is one of the fastest-growing United Methodist churches in the country. It started by creating its traditional worship format in such a way that it spoke to the people they were trying to reach. In the first years of its formation, it didn't need to create a new format because what it was doing was effective. When one worship experience overflowed with people, they added another worship experience. Today, they offer four traditional worship experiences on Sunday mornings. For them, new options meant offering the same worship experience at different times. Five years ago, they added a contemporary worship that meets on Saturday evenings. Three years ago, they added a contemporary worship that meets on Sunday evenings. As of February of 2000, they averaged more than 5,400 in worship.

Each church defines what is meant by traditional and contemporary. For Church of the Resurrection, the traditional experience includes choirs, hymns from *The United Methodist Hymnal,* and multimedia used during the sermon. The contemporary experience includes a praise band, contemporary Christian music, and multimedia used during the sermon.

A congregation may also create a new worship experience to meet the needs of a particular people group. Bau Dang, the lead pastor at Wesley United Methodist Church in San Diego, found out that a large number of his Vietnamese congregation worked on Sundays. Most were men who worked in restaurants and in the retail business. In order to meet their need for worship, the church started a service at six on Sunday mornings. The setting for this worship experience for working parents is a fellowship/instruction group, whose single focus is to meet the needs of a group of people with specific circumstances.

By creating a new option, Bau Dang's church was able to accomplish two important goals: First, it met the critical need of a new group to have a worship experience. This service allowed workers, usually about forty to sixty people, to attend worship before going to work. Second, the new worship service allowed the men and their families to share a common worship experience on Sundays, even though the families of the men also attended the worship experience at eleven on Sunday mornings.

The new worship experience at Wesley United Methodist Church was started not just so that the congregation could add a new style of worship. Rather, it was started to meet the needs of a distinct people group: working parents whose employment circumstances offered them no opportunity to worship and therefore caused them to become increasingly disenfranchised from the church and from their families.

The reason this service works is that Wesley United Methodist Church already has a celebrative-worship service that averages more than 300 at the eleven o'clock service. Remember, a celebrative worship of 120 or more allows more people of a greater diversity to participate. When a congregation has a celebrative-worship experience firmly established, it is in a good position to create other worship opportunities of different sizes to meet other kinds of needs.

Wesley United Methodist Church also offers an English-language service to meet the needs of members who were there before the Vietnamese ministry was started. It also includes people of Vietnamese descent who wish to worship in English. Additionally, the congregation has a strong small-group discipleship system where people learn and practice the basic spiritual disciplines of the Christian faith.

Existing congregations wishing to start new worship experiences should, like Bau Dang, ask some key questions:

■ Is there a group of people in the community who are not able to come to worship at the time of the congregation's current worship service?

■ Is there a new people group in town for whom new small groups and a new worship service can be offered?

■ Is there a generational group that does not attend the current worship service for whom a different style and format of worship would be attractive?

9.3. Wesley UMC

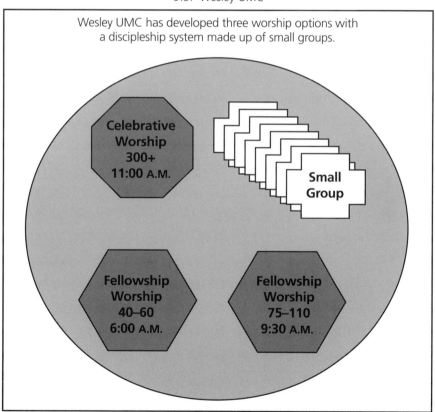

As the Ephesian faith community launched its public ministry, it entered into a bold new enterprise: telling the whole community about Jesus Christ. As people heard the message, they were called to become followers of Jesus Christ and to enter into a process of spiritual growth and maturity that would transform their lives and transform the community in which they lived.

The Ephesian believers did not enter into this new stage of ministry lightly. Through much prayer, reflection, and preparation, they went forward, trusting God for their witness. Today, each congregation has to decide whom it is called to serve. Congregations that have experienced the grace of God are challenged to proclaim the message of Jesus Christ to the people groups that surround them. Like those who were a part of the faith community in Ephesus, God calls each of us to be a witness to the saving grace of Jesus Christ.

Endnotes

1 Based on *Report to the Global Evangelism Consultative Meeting,* by Rev. Geoffrey Kagoro, June 1999.

Chapter Ten

EXPERIENCE- BASED WORSHIP

When Bishop Robert E. Fannin of the North Alabama Annual Conference was told about the new "Cappuccino and Christ" worship experience at First United Methodist Church in Huntsville, he asked why it couldn't be called the "Christ and Cappuccino" service. When the congregation's leaders ran the request by the public relations company that had been helping them in their marketing, the company said, "You have to start with cappuccino. People in the community know what cappuccino is; they don't know who Christ is."

A s we move into the first decade of the twenty-first century, new approaches need to be offered to speak to people who increasingly operate out of an experience-based mentality. People with wide access to information about a wide variety of religions, religious beliefs, and spiritual modalities come to a worship experience with a different set of assumptions than people did in the past. Most people do not see themselves as unbelievers, secular people, or even as seekers; they see themselves as believers. They may not be Christian believers, but in their minds they are believers in something.

As they come to a church, they are looking to find out what the church has to teach them about the Christian faith and how the church can help them learn more about their spirituality. They are not coming to adopt a new set of beliefs; instead, they are coming to be part of a conversation.

You may think that the best strategy would be to water down what you have to offer, in order to make it easier to digest, but the opposite is true. What people are looking for is what makes your faith community stand out from the rest, what is distinctive about its flavor.

Today, people participate because they are having an experience of the presence of God. By creating settings that move people closer to God, growing congregations offer spiritual experiences that speak to the heart.

Looking at the World Differently

Four ways of looking at the world help us understand how people's ways of processing information have been shaped by living in the world of electronic media. The first way of processing information is *surfing*. Instead of immersing themselves in one option, they move freely among many different experiences, much as a person surfs through TV channels to find a program to watch. As a result, people find themselves floating from one experience to the next without going deeply into one experience because a better one might be around the corner. Having multiple options breeds a desire for the new.

A second way of processing information is *matrix thinking*. Matrix thinking interweaves a variety of sources of information at the same time. Think of the experience of watching a music video. The music video combines music and sensory material to create an artistic expression that is filled with many different images and sounds. In matrix thinking, a person is able to process many different images and sounds at the same time. Those who have grown up on video games, the Internet, and music videos have developed this skill of processing a number of different things at the same time.

A third way of processing information is *iconic thinking*. Iconic thinking is focused on symbols or icons that contain layers of information and meaning. The "swoosh" symbol of Nike shoes is an icon of the Nike experience. So effective is this icon that all Nike has to do is put a swoosh symbol on a billboard and you will know what it is all about. This possibility is the reason companies invest so much money in their trademarks. Think of some of these that you see daily—NBC's peacock, CBS's eye, Disney's Mickey Mouse ears, Coca-Cola's bottle, the music that is played when the Intel Inside logo is displayed in Intel computer commercials. Rather than being dependent on the written word, iconic thinking collapses many messages into one symbol.

A fourth way of processing information that is particularly relevant for those who design worship for people in their early twenties and younger is *interactivity*. Rather then passive listening,

Millennials want to be active learners. Rather than education as an individual pursuit, learning happens through the interaction of the group and through interactive media. Rather than responding to the top-down media of broadcast television, Millennials thrive on interaction. This pattern repeats itself in education as well. Rather than the teacher telling the students the facts of history, teachers will increasingly move to creating environments where the students can discover the facts for themselves. When computers first came into the public view, it was thought that children would use them to mindlessly do math programs over and over again, like training a rat to go through a maze. Instead, with the development of the Internet, the computer becomes a portal to an information-rich world where students collaborate with other students to make discoveries for themselves.

By combining these four ways of thinking—surfing, matrix thinking, iconic thinking, and interactivity—we begin to get a picture of the way people process information. The one word that captures what is going on is *experience*. What attracts the interactive/matrix-thinking/iconic/culture-surfer is an experience that causes him or her to dig deeper to the truth. While many people see the world in this way, Postmoderns and Millennials increasingly operate exclusively out of this framework.

The Experience Economy

While much focus in the business world has been on information technologies and the service industry, we are moving into an experience-based economy in which experiences have economic value. Today, companies are less concerned with the product they are making or even the service they are offering in support of the product. Instead, they are looking at the experience that is produced from owning or using their product.

When every car on the market has four wheels, a steering wheel, and a seat for the driver to sit in, the components that are added to make it your car are what differentiates one car from another. Color, size, audio equipment, and ease of handling are all factors that create the car you want to drive. While all cars have the same fundamental purpose of being an individualized transportation device, what is important to the buyer and owner of the car is the way it reflects and enhances his or her lifestyle. When all these factors are put together, the driver has a certain experience that may or may not be favorable. Car manufacturers want you to have such a powerfully positive experience of owning the car that you will come back for an updated model when you are ready to buy another car.

Take a cup of coffee—why are people willing to pay two to four dollars for coffee at a coffee house when they can make the same coffee for far less at home? It's because coffee drinkers want more than simply a cup of coffee. What gets coffee drinkers to part with their money is the experience that is offered when they receive and drink the coffee in a special environment.

Entertailment

Retailers have come to realize that when a memorable experience is wrapped around the purchase of a product, people are willing to pay more money for the product. This understanding of the way people think is so pervasive that the retail business is creating a whole new way of selling products. Entertailment is a synthesis between entertainment and retail. In entertailment, the experience that is offered is more important than the product that is being sold. To say it another way, the product is an icon of an experience. The product—toy, T-shirt, CD, or whatever—brings back the memories of the experience.

When I discussed this concept with a group of youth workers, one woman excitedly raised her hand and exclaimed, "Now I get it!" When I inquired further, the woman said that one of the girls in her youth group had made a quilt from all the T-shirts the girl had collected over the years. The teenager showed the quilt to the woman and said, "This is my life." For this young person, the T-shirts were icons that reminded her of meaningful experiences that shaped her understanding of the world.

You have probably experienced the phenomenon of entertailment without even knowing it. Increasingly, retail stores are adopting the experience-based philosophy of entertailment to sell products. Barnes & Noble bookstores make sales by creating the atmosphere of an elite men's club where one can discuss the great ideas of the day in plush surroundings that include leather chairs and a coffee house. It also is a place where you can browse through books at your leisure, as if you were in a library. At the end of the experience, you almost feel obligated to pay your dues by purchasing a book.

Oshman's Sporting Goods, which sells sports equipment and clothing, is putting basketball courts in its stores, so that customers can play a game of basketball there.

MARS The Musician's Planet, a chain of music stores, has created a huge music store where customers are encouraged to try out the music instruments. As you enter the drum section, a rack of ear muffs hangs at the entrance to the enclosed area, encouraging you to protect your ears by covering them.

It is no accident that Disney Stores have a huge pile of stuffed animals right in front of the wall-sized video screen. As children watch their favorite characters sing and dance, they are encouraged to take the experience home with them in the form of Winnie the Pooh or Bambi.

We see this practice of entertailment in other places as well. Customers of the Hard Rock Café faithfully purchase T-shirts, which they wear as a way to tell people that they have been to the Hard Rock Café in locations around the world. Attendees at rock concerts and Broadway musicals are encouraged to take home programs, T-shirts, and CD's. Fans of sports teams are invited to buy the home team's jersey, so that they can wear the number of their favorite player.

Even the travel industry is getting onboard with this trend by offering retirees travel experiences that are more than a vacation. The travel industry is finding that their best customers are those who want to learn new things, so they are developing travel packages that immerse travelers in a new culture and environment. For instance, travelers can experience firsthand what is was like living in Florence during the Renaissance or in Egypt when the pyramids were built.

Memorable Experiences Are More Than Entertailment

But entertailment is just one piece of a larger picture. The way to attract and keep guests is to provide a memorable experience. In their book *The Experience Economy: Work Is Theatre and Every Business a Stage*, B. Joseph Pine II and James H. Gilmore make a distinction between entertaining customers and engaging them. When you simply entertain guests, you do not ask for their active participation. Instead, they are invited to watch and observe. After a while, they tire of the same old thing and look for other forms of entertainment. To enrich an experience, you have to take a look not only at entertainment but also at the esthetic, the educational, and the escapist aspects of the experience. Pine and Gilmore flesh this out by saying, "When designing your experience, you should consider the following questions:

- "What can be done to improve the *esthetics* of the experience? The esthetics are what make your guests want to come in, sit down, and hang out. Think about what you can do to make the environment more inviting, interesting, or comfortable. You want to create an atmosphere in which your guests feel free 'to be.'
- "Once there, what should your guests do? The *escapist* aspect of an experience draws your guests further, immersing them in activities. Focus on what you should encourage guests 'to do' if they are to become active participants in the experience.
- "The *educational* aspect of an experience, like the escapist, is essentially active. Learning, as it is now largely understood, requires the full participation of the learner. What do you want your guests 'to learn' from the experience? What information or activities will help to engage them in the exploration of knowledge and skills?
- "*Entertainment,* like esthetics, is a passive aspect of an experience. When your guests are entertained, they're not really doing anything but responding to (enjoying, laughing at, etc.) the experience. Professional speakers lace their speeches with jokes to hold the attention of their audience, to get them to listen to the ideas. What can you do...to get your guests 'to stay'? How can you make the experience more fun and more enjoyable"[1]

10.1. Four Aspects of an Experience

Esthetics—What do you want people to be?
Escapist—What do you want people to do?
Educational—What do you want people to learn?
Entertainment—How do you get people to stay?
Based on *The Experience Economy: Work Is Theatre and Every Business a Stage,* by B. Joseph Pine II and James H. Gilmore (Boston: Harvard Business School Press, 1999), pages 39–40.

For a moment, use these four aspects of an experience as a lens through which to view the last worship experience you attended.

- What was it that helped you get in touch with God? What allowed you to be yourself in your relationship with the holy?
- What were you asked to do? Did these things enhance or take away from the experience?
- What did you learn? What were you invited to do that helped you go deeper into your relationship with Jesus, to those around you, and to the creation?
- What caused you to stay—habit, respect, or courtesy toward those in leadership? Or was it an experience that was so compelling you did not want to miss out on what happened next?

Experiences Are Transformational

The natural outcome of meaningful experiences is the transformation of the person who has had the experience. The reason worship is a critical part in the life of faith for a believer is that worship changes us. Through the experience of worship, we are drawn closer to God; we are challenged to love one another; and we are called be in ministry, to go into all the world telling of the joy of knowing Jesus Christ.

The artful combination of music, Word, sacrament, and interaction with fellow worshipers creates a life-changing experience that compels us to desire an even deeper experience of God. Worship is not simply an experience or a learning event or a time for fellowship. At its best, worship moves the believer forward and deeper into the life of faith.

The Ephesian Church Changed People's Lives

Two years after the launching of the public ministry in Ephesus, a number of dramatic occurrences took place. Magicians in the city were so convicted by the preaching of Paul and the witness of the Christians that they took all their magic books and scrolls and burned them in the center of the city. This was no small thing. Ephesus was such a center of magic that the ancient world used the term *Ephesia grammata* (Ephesian writings) to describe special documents that contained spells and magic formulas. These scrolls contained names of gods who promised to protect the wearers of amulets or lockets that contained these magic names.[2] Acts 19:19 tells us that the estimated value of the burned items was fifty thousand silver coins.

A few days after the public burning of the magic books, a riot broke out. Led by Demetrius, a silversmith who made silver shrines of Artemis, the silversmiths blamed the growing Christian movement for ruining their business. In Acts 19:25-27, Demetrius says:

> Men, you know that we get our wealth from this business. You also see and hear that not only in Ephesus but in almost the whole of Asia this Paul has persuaded and drawn away a considerable number of people by saying that gods made with hands are not gods. And there is danger not only that this trade of ours may come into disrepute but also that the temple of the great goddess Artemis will be scorned, and she will be deprived of her majesty that brought all Asia and the world to worship her.

So many people were being transformed by the power of the gospel of Jesus Christ that it threatened one of the most profitable businesses in the city: the sale of idols of Artemis. This account in Acts brings home a central point that we cannot overlook: The experience of the grace and power of Jesus Christ changes the way people live.

Transformation Happens Through a Series of Experiences

Transformation that truly changes a person happens as a result of a series of experiences that form and guide. Pine and Gilmore's statement here should give every congregational leader something to think about:

> By staging a series of experiences, companies are better able to achieve a lasting effect on the buyer than through an isolated event. It is the revisiting of a recurring theme, experienced through distinct and yet unified events, that transforms.[3]

While the church may see itself as one of the prime places where people are transformed, Pine and Gilmore's audience is business. Their contention is that companies who learn how to develop experiences that communicate deeper to customers are the ones who will be on the forefront of creating a new economic model based on the ability of companies to transform their customers' lives.

What companies could benefit from this approach? What about a fitness club? Is not their goal the transformation of an individual? A fitness club that truly is focused on transformation will help their customer develop a diet and exercise plan that will help the customer get to and stay at their correct weight. It will develop an individualized exercise program that develops strong muscles for endurance and promotes a healthy lifestyle that will last a lifetime. The ultimate goal is for an individual to have a long, healthy life. How much would you be willing to pay a fitness club that can deliver on that promise to you?

What makes a faith community different from a place where worship happens is that people are transformed. Churches should take this principle to heart. The goal is not simply to put on a good worship experience. The goal is to create worship experiences that are linked to a discipleship system through which participants grow and develop as disciples of Jesus Christ. The point is that what makes a worship experience effective is not the "label on the box." Effectiveness is determined by what is happening with the people in a faith community as they worship God. Are they growing in faith? Are they living a Christian lifestyle? Are they discovering their spiritual gifts for ministry? Are they practicing their spiritual disciplines? Are they reaching out to new people in the name of Christ? Are they creating healthy relationships? Are newcomers giving their lives to Christ?

If these things are happening in your church, you will have no problem attracting new people to your church. The Spirit of God will bring the growth. But if these things are not happening, your planning for the worship experience may require a new approach. Rather than starting with the worship planners, you have to start with the people who are coming to the worship experience. This approach requires a different mindset and a different set of tools.

The Overall Worship Format

As congregations create new worship experiences, they have to make decisions about two different stages of development: First, they have to choose the overall format of the worship experience that is going to be offered on a weekly basis. Second, they have to create the individual worship experiences week by week.

In most congregations, the same basic worship elements are used for a worship experience that are offered at a specific time each week. For example, the worship experience at eleven on Sunday morning will be framed around a series of expectations and shared assumptions that both the worship leaders and the worshipers have come to regard as what is normative for that worship experience. This normative pattern may be changed when another element is introduced on a regular basis (for example, when Holy Communion is celebrated in this same worship time on the first Sunday of the month). Allowances for other changes happen when special experiences are offered, such as a Youth Sunday or a Christmas cantata.

These normative worship elements are combined to create the basic worship format of a given worship experience. Each worship experience has its own flavor and appeal by virtue of the elements that are used.

By using the worship matrix (page 148), you can create different worship experiences by combining different elements. The worship matrix identifies eight basic elements that are commonly used in different worship formats.

Common to all worship experiences are *proclamation* and *Scripture*. Proclamation may happen through preaching, but it also may happen through drama or storytelling. Proclamation is the articulation of the Word of God to a specific people group at a specific time. A key role of proclamation is to cast the vision of what this community of faith is to become as it follows Jesus Christ. Scripture is a key component of the proclamation as it states the core values of the Christian faith.

Historic hymns are the shared traditions and music that have been handed down from generation to generation. The singing of historic hymns is a reminder of the faith of those who have come before. Singing these hymns also helps worshipers form shared memories of the way God has worked in the past.

10.2. Worship Matrix

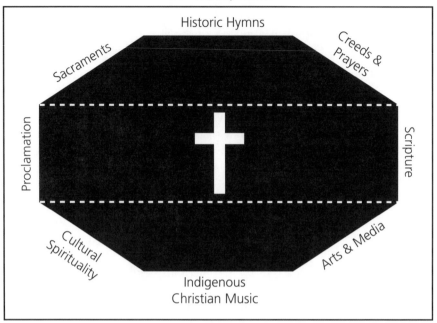

Historic Hymns
Sacraments
Creeds & Prayers
Proclamation
Scripture
Cultural Spirituality
Arts & Media
Indigenous Christian Music

Indigenous Christian music ties directly to the cultural norms of the people group for whom the worship experience is designed. This is a key distinction that is missed sometimes when it comes to the discussion about music. Much of the current battles in churches over music, music instrumentation, and the types of musicians who play in worship experiences revolve around one issue: Does the music speak in the heart language of the people?

In 1986, Jack and Jo Popjes reached a roadblock in their ministry with the Canela people of northeastern Brazil. As much as they tried, they could not decipher the intricacies of the Canela music. In a moment of inspiration, they turned to Dr. Tom Avery, a Wycliffe ethnomusicologist who was based in Belém, Brazil. The first thing Avery did was to dissuade them from simply translating hymns into the Canela language and playing the original European/American music. Many times, this approach ends up with unintended consequences. For example, if an indigenous culture associates high notes with sadness, then a hymn such as "He Lives" would make little sense. They would wonder why the resurrection of Jesus would bring such sadness.

Through a year of research, Avery was able to study the Canela music system. One of the most important things he learned was that

Canelas use a different interval between notes than Westerners use. Therefore, Canela music could not be played on a piano, because notes would fall between the cracks.

Working together with the Popjes, Avery created twenty-three Canela songs with Christian lyrics, most of which were direct quotations from Scripture. When they played the music for the Canelas, the response was dramatic. One Canela song leader responded, "I never realized we could make up our own songs. I tried once years before, but no one would sing it. What's more, (these new songs) are about God, and I want to sing about God."[4]

Another Canela brought home an important point when she spoke to Jack and Jo Popjes, who had been with them for almost twenty years: "You have been here all these years and all you gave us was writing. Your friend Tom has only been here a little while, and he taught us how to sing to God."[5]

Tom Avery's work with different people groups has brought him to this important conclusion: "Whenever a church is born, music is involved. Using local music puts the Word of God into a form the people already know and use."[6]

Rather than using the words *contemporary* or *traditional,* a better term to use is *indigenous,* which means that the music comes from the people and speaks to them in a form that they already understand.

The word *sacraments* refers to Holy Communion and baptism—the shared experiences of the Christian faith that reiterate and dramatize the core beliefs of Christianity. Baptism is the public proclamation that a person belongs to God through Jesus Christ. When infants and children are baptized, the congregation makes a commitment to do all in their power to create a place where the infants and children can grow in faith and experience the love of God. When an adult is baptized, he or she makes a public proclamation of a decision to follow Jesus Christ. Through this sacrament, people—children or adults—are incorporated into the Christian community. When the crowd at Pentecost asked Peter what they should do, he replied: "Repent, and be baptized every one of you in the name of Jesus Christ so that your sins may be forgiven; and you will receive the gift of the Holy Spirit" (Acts 2:38). Baptism comes with a promise: When you give your life to Jesus Christ, you are filled with the Holy Spirit. Baptism is also at the heart of what unites us as Christians. Whether lay or clergy, all who are baptized are gifted for ministry.

At the beginning of the Christian movement, the Lord's Supper was at the heart of worship. In 1 Corinthians 11, Paul focuses on the importance of the Lord's Supper in the life of the faith community.

> For I received from the Lord what I also handed on to you, that the Lord Jesus on the night when he was betrayed took a loaf of bread, and when he had given thanks, he broke it and said, "This is my body that is for you. Do this in remembrance of me." In the same way he took the cup also, after supper, saying, "This cup in the new covenant in my blood. Do this, as often as you drink it, in remembrance of me." For as often as you eat this bread and drink the cup, you proclaim the Lord's death until he comes. (1 Corinthians 11:23-26)

In the act of taking the body and blood of Jesus Christ, we remember his sacrifice on our behalf and proclaim to the world that through Jesus Christ we have new life. For the early Methodists, taking the Lord's Supper served as a means of grace; through that act, people were forgiven of sins and brought deeper into the mystery of following Jesus Christ.

Creeds and Prayers are gifts passed down to us through history. The Apostles' Creed and the Lord's Prayer are examples of this body of work that forms the Christian memory of what we believe and what we are called to do as followers of Jesus Christ.

Arts and Media are the various forms of artistic expression that are used in worship. Like music, arts and media are indigenous to the culture of the people groups that form the worshiping congregation. Dance, drama, graphics, paintings, anthems, videos, and/or stained glass are all ways people can use art to express their faith.

Cultural spirituality refers to spiritual stories and songs of the culture that are redeemed in the context of a Christian worship service. For example, at one worship service I showed a video clip from the movie *Homeward Bound: The Incredible Journey*, a movie about two dogs and a cat who travel across the country to find their home. The last scene shows them finally making it home to their owners. As I looked at the faces of people in the congregation, I saw that some actually had tears in their eyes. The message for the day focused on what it means to come home. Whenever people in that congregation see that movie, they will now see it through the eyes of the gospel and will connect the story with their own spiritual journey. This is what the word *redeeming* means. Popular songs, stories, video clips, and other sources of information contain within them spiritual content that, when used in worship, help people connect their faith with everyday living. (You must get permission to show video clips. See page 171 for information about obtaining permission.)

Creating Different Worship Options

By mixing and matching these basic elements, different worship options can be designed that offer different worship experiences that meet the needs of different people groups. For example, a congregation may offer one worship experience where the primary elements are proclamation and Scripture, historic hymns, creeds and prayers, and arts and media. The primary musical instrumentation may be piano and organ. A second worship experience may be offered that contains proclamation and Scripture, indigenous Christian music, sacraments, and cultural spirituality. The primary music instrumentation for this service may be a praise band. A third worship experience may be one that uses proclamation and Scripture, cultural spirituality, and sacraments. String instruments and the choir may be the main source of music for this service.

Recently, I was talking with a pastor whose congregation was contemplating starting a worship experience that would be designed as an arena experience. Icons of famous sporting events would be placed in the sanctuary. At times, members would be asked to push giant balls down the aisle. Video clips and stories from sports would be used as illustrations in messages. The indigenous motif of the experience would be sports and all the dynamics that go with it. This worship experience would be using proclamation and Scripture, cultural spirituality (sports, in this case), arts and media, and indigenous Christian music.

To say that the above-mentioned worship experiences are traditional or contemporary would miss the mark. Instead, they contain elements of worship that create a unique experience of God that resonates with a specific group of people.

These descriptions are a small sample of the kinds of worship experiences that can be created. The way to plan your worship service is to gather a group of people who will be attending the worship experience. Discuss with them the various elements of worship and then determine which elements are nonnegotiable for them. In other words, the service would not be worship for them without certain elements.

A member of a church told me about a group of people sixty-five years and older who had started a new worship experience at a retirement home. When I asked him what kind of music they were singing, he said they were singing "The Old Rugged Cross," "Amazing Grace," and "In the Garden." For this group, these hymns are their heart music, their indigenous music—music of the faith that best expresses their worship of God. Particular historic hymns, which they had grown up with and heard since their childhood, were vital to them. For this group, these songs would be a nonnegotiable element in their worship service.

At another church, a new worship service started at 8:45 A.M. As the core group wrestled with the worship format, they identified two key elements: contemporary Christian music and Holy Communion. For them, the contemporary Christian music was their indigenous music.

Theme-Based Worship

Having determined the normative elements that will be used for a given worship experience (8:30 A.M. or 11:00 A.M.), the next step is to create the worship experiences that will be offered each week. This is the place where the real fun begins. The challenge is to create an engaging experience each week without losing sight of the effect the ongoing experience of coming to worship week after week is having on the participants. The critical question to ask is, Will the cumulative effect of coming to worship on an ongoing basis be transformational?

A theme-based approach to worship is key to communicating to people today because it forces the worship planner to take seriously the experience that is being created: *How does the Scripture apply to the lives of the people who are in my congregation?* Even more important: *How does the Scripture apply to me?* What people long for is something that is real for real people who struggle as they do with the demands of the gospel.

In theme-based worship, everything that happens in the worship experience is part of the message. Regardless of the worship format (whatever elements you use in your worship experience), what ties it together is the theme for that service. This is true whether you call your worship experience traditional, contemporary, classic, or new song. What attracts and keeps people coming back is a message that uses the various elements in a worship experience to communicate the gospel.

To say this another way, the sermon is just one part of the message. Everything else that happens—hymns, songs, Scripture readings, sacraments, and so forth—is also part of the message. Everything that happens in the worship experience creates the message for that day.

Creating Theme-Based Worship

To plan theme-based worship, start by articulating a question that will point people to the theme of the worship experience. To determine the question, begin with the Scripture text that will be used as part of the message. Ask: "What question or life issue does the Scripture illuminate? What is the human condition that the Scripture addresses?"

Take, for instance, 1 Corinthians 9:24-27:

> Do you not know that in a race the runners all compete, but only one receives the prize? Run in such a way that you may win it. Athletes exercise self-control in all things; they do it to receive a perishable wreath, but we an imperishable one. So I do not run aimlessly, nor do I box as though beating the air; but I punish my body and enslave it, so that after proclaiming to others I myself should not be disqualified.

What is the main issue that is being addressed? For the sake of illustration, let's say that the main life issue the passage raises is, "What are you chasing after?" Or, put differently, "Does your life have purpose?" So the theme for this worship experience, which is based on 1 Corinthians 9:24-27, might be "Through faith in Jesus Christ, your life has purpose."

Next, identify the indigenous motif that is used in the context of the Scripture. Images, icons, and illustrations can be identified and used throughout the worship experience, both in song and in other media. In this instance, the Scripture uses the motif of running a race. By using images and illustrations of running a race, the Scripture can be brought alive.

If the worship were based on Jesus' conversation with the woman at the well, the theme might be "Jesus offers you living water." The question might be "Why are you not satisfied?" The indigenous motif would be the well. Images and illustrations based on water, thirst, and drinking could be used. What would it be like to enter the worship area and find a variety of drinking glasses, mugs, and cups on the altar or put in alcoves of windows? Or what about images of water projected on a screen as people enter?

Once you identify the theme, the main question, and the indigenous motif, you can create a worship service around these things. To build the worship experience, start by looking for media that raises the main question identified. Media refers to a wide variety of ways of communicating: a mini-drama, a story, a video clip, a dance, or a song. For example, the question for 1 Corinthians 9:24-27 could be raised by showing a video clip from the movie *Forest Gump.* Use the scene where a group of runners is following Forest as he runs across the country. In a climactic scene, Forest stops and walks away from the crowd. The crowd exclaims, "Where are you going? What are we supposed to do now?" For the worship experience, this sets the stage as the preacher asks, "Where are you going? What or who are you chasing after?" (You must get permission to show video clips. See page 171 for information about obtaining permission.)

Another way to raise the question might be through a children's message. Once the children have assembled at the front of the worship space, have everyone take off one shoe and hold it up. Ask a couple of the children to tell you what kind of shoe he or she is wearing. Then hold up a running shoe and ask, "What kind of shoe is this?" After the children respond, ask, "When we wear this kind of shoe, where are we going?"

After identifying the media or illustration that is going to be used to raise the question, consider what media can be used to echo the theme after the proclamation. The media might be a hymn such as "When We Walk With the Lord" or "Thy Word," or a popular song such as "Bridge Over Troubled Water." (Remember to get permission from the copyright holder if you plan to print the words. See page 171 for information about obtaining permission.)

The proclamation is nestled between these two forms of media that first ask the question and then echo the theme after the proclamation. The focus of the proclamation is to articulate a response to the main question that has been asked in the theme.

After identifying each of these key elements, add them to the plan for the whole worship experience. Keep in mind that everything is part of the message. Look carefully at each element of the experience to see how you can bring the theme alive.

10.3. Identifying and Using the Theme

- Identify the theme and question based on Scripture.
  (Theme: "Through faith in Jesus Christ, your life has purpose" 1 Corinthians 9:24-27.)
  (Question: "Does your life have purpose?")
- Identify the indigenous motif (running a race).
- Find media (drama, video, song, story, and so forth) to raise the question (scene of runners in the movie *Forest Gump*).
- Find media (drama, video, song, story, and so forth) that echoes the theme ("Thy Word").
- Develop a sermon that responds to the question.

Worship as Drama

A theme-based worship service may be presented in the experience-based format of drama. Such an experience follows two basic principles: First, everything that happens in the worship experience is part of the message. Second, using elements that are indigenous to the people group to whom the experience is offered allows the faith community to reach out and receive them into the Christian community.

The dramatic form is a variation of the Basic Pattern of Worship (*The United Methodist Hymnal*, page 2). The Basic Pattern contains four elements: Entrance, Proclamation and Response, Thanksgiving, and Sending Forth. Like the fourfold pattern of the Basic Pattern of Worship, each act of a drama has its own purpose. (See "10.4. Worship as Drama," on page 156.)

Act I: Gathering

Like the Entrance in the Basic Pattern, the Gathering time in the dramatic form invites participants into the presence of God. The difference is that in the dramatic form, the Gathering starts the moment someone drives into your church's parking lot. Studies show that people make decisions about whether to come back to a church based on what happens in the first five to ten minutes after they arrive. The decision is made before the first song is sung or the sermon is preached. The ease of finding a parking place, locating where the worship experience is taking place, finding childcare, being welcomed by other worshipers—all inform the newcomer about what this faith community is like. This Gathering time is part of the worship experience.

From the moment people enter the worship area, the theme is stated. Everything present in the worship area is a medium for the theme. Whatever you can see, touch, smell, taste, and hear is a medium. The worship bulletin (if one is used) is a medium. How does the cover on the bulletin illustrate the theme? The decorations on the altar, banners, and other decorations help people identify with the theme. Remember that icons convey meaning. What would a pair of running shoes on the altar convey?

If you plan to have Holy Communion, what kind of bread would carry the theme? One of the most meaningful images at a worship experience I attended on Pentecost Sunday was one in which a wide variety of breads was offered at Communion. The message focused on how people from all over the world were gathered together on the Day of Pentecost and were called to follow Jesus. The different types of bread became the illustration of the different cultures of the

10.4. Worship as Drama

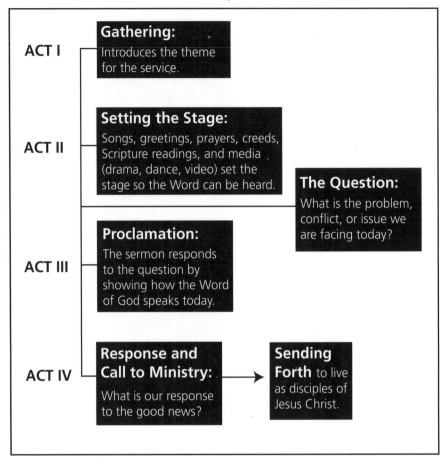

ACT I — **Gathering:** Introduces the theme for the service.

ACT II — **Setting the Stage:** Songs, greetings, prayers, creeds, Scripture readings, and media (drama, dance, video) set the stage so the Word can be heard.

The Question: What is the problem, conflict, or issue we are facing today?

ACT III — **Proclamation:** The sermon responds to the question by showing how the Word of God speaks today.

ACT IV — **Response and Call to Ministry:** What is our response to the good news? → **Sending Forth** to live as disciples of Jesus Christ.

world. Pita bread, rye bread, wheat bread, and torrito chips were used to bring home the point. During the whole worship experience, the different types of bread were spread across the altar.

The worship service begins when the worship leader introduces the theme. This can be done through a call to worship, a song or hymn, or a welcoming remark such as: "I don't know about you, but I have been running around like crazy this week. I'm ready to turn my eyes to God. Will you join me in prayer?"

Act II: Setting the Stage

Setting the Stage in the dramatic form serves as a bridge between the Entrance and the Proclamation and Response of the Basic Pattern. It prepares people to hear the Word of God by using elements that are indigenous to the culture. This is the point where the format of worship shows its variety. Robert Webber, in *Planning Blended Worship: The Creative Mixture of Old and New*, says:

> While the content of worship (the gospel) is nonnegotiable and the fourfold pattern of worship is strongly recommended, the style of worship is subject to considerable variety. This is because worshiping styles are rooted in the ever-changing kaleidoscope of human culture. There is no one style of worship that is suitable for all people always and everywhere. Instead, the style of worship will differ according to time and place relative to the changing patterns of culture.[7]

Immediately, worship moves into Act II: Setting the Stage. Using a mix of songs, greetings, prayers, creeds, Scripture readings, and other media, the stage is set so that the Word can be heard. It is at this point that the normative elements that make this worship experience distinctive are used. If creeds and prayers are used, this is where they are placed. If a series of praise songs are sung, this is where they are sung. Like the telling of a story, this is where you show that you identify with who has come to worship. You start with where they are.

Because most visitors arrive right at the time worship begins, what happens first communicates a lot about the nature of the faith community. You may notice that a movie that is scheduled to start at 4:30 usually starts at 4:40. People are used to having a little slack time when they arrive.

If people walk into the worship area in the middle of announcements or a prayer, they may feel uncomfortable—like they are interrupting what is happening. Think of what you can do at the beginning of the worship experience that will help visitors to walk right in and not feel uncomfortable. Personally, I like to have two or three songs sung at the beginning of the worship experience. This allows people to walk into the midst of the worshiping community without being put on the spot, and it sets the mood for the worship experience. Use your creativity, keeping in mind how to invite newcomers into the worship experience.

In worship, the setting-the-stage period draws people into the worship experience. It moves them to a point where they are receptive to hearing the message for the day.

The Question

At the bridge point between Act II and Act III, the question of the day is brought forward. As was stated earlier, the question may be asked in a number of ways. When the question is asked, the theme is stated clearly in a way that is easily identified by the congregation. Just as in a movie, novel, or play, it is when the question is asked that whatever conflict that exists is brought out into the open. It is at this point that the obstacles are clearly seen and tension builds.

One of the keys to communicating to people is the need to be real. So, at this point in the service, articulate the real issues with which people are struggling. Life problems and questions that emerge out of the Scripture need to be stated and the question asked: "What does God have to say about this?" Drama, video, stories, or songs are forms that work well at this point in the service.

Act III: Proclamation

Proclamation in the dramatic form corresponds with Proclamation and Response in the Basic Pattern. Here the focus is on relational preaching, proclamation that helps people live the Christian faith in daily life.

The sermon responds to the main question for the service by showing how the Word of God speaks to the question. This is where the meaning of the experience is articulated. Again, the sermon may be given in a variety of forms, but it should be in a form that is normative for the worship experience that is being offered. It is the responsibility of the preacher or those who are doing the Proclamation to wrap up the loose ends and draw in what has happened before in the worship experience. In the case of the *Forest Gump* example, the preacher would refer to the illustration, link it to the Scripture, and use it as a springboard to talk about purpose and meaning.

Act IV: Response and Call to Ministry

Response and Call to Ministry and Sending Forth correspond with Thanksgiving as a response to the Word and Sending Forth in the Basic Pattern. In this part of the service, the congregation is called to respond to God and to all that has happened in the worship experience. The Lord's Supper, baptism, an invitational prayer, a special reading, an invitation to give one's life to Christ, and/or offering can call people to respond to God.

Sending Forth comes as part of the people's response to God's Word. Worshipers are sent forth to live as disciples of Jesus Christ. A song, a hymn, and/or a blessing or benediction can be used. It is at this point that you can use media that echoes the theme.

Worship-Planning Teams

Offering theme-based worship experiences takes a team of people working together. Gone are the days when the pastor designed the worship service for the congregation. To touch the heart of the members of the faith community, to walk where the people walk, takes more than one set of eyes. Worship leaders need to involve other people in planning worship.

One way to involve others is to gather a group of people to meet monthly for the purpose of identifying themes and wrestling with issues that are important in the faith community and in the wider community where the church is located. By using Scripture and identifying key issues, this team can help to shape the service. This group can be the same as the one that puts the week-to-week worship together, or it can be another group made up of key leaders from the congregation who will communicate with those who plan.

One way to configure this is to see this group as the preaching team. The preaching team's responsibility is to identify a theme that supports and builds the vision of the church for each worship experience. Some congregations have moved to a place where the actual preaching is done by a preaching team, while the pastor shares the preaching responsibility with other staff and members of the congregation. This is especially true in congregations such as Christ Church in Ft. Lauderdale, Florida, where two worship experiences are offered at the same time. One person cannot do both worship experiences, so the members of the preaching team use the same theme for all the worship experiences offered during that week. This coordination ensures that even though the format of worship may be different, the theme unites the congregation as it focuses the whole congregation on the core values and vision of the church. The congregation is united not by the outward forms of worship but by the core values that are experienced in worship.

As part of this process, a congregation can form a culture surfers team. This team's role is to help identify media that illustrate the themes identified by the preaching team. Every congregation has someone who loves to read novels, someone who collects videos, someone who listens to music and the radio, and someone who watches television. Critical to the success of this process is giving people the themes for the worship experiences way in advance. The worship leader gives these individuals the upcoming worship themes and asks them to collect illustrations that can be used in the worship experience. These individuals then meet at regular intervals to discuss their ideas. When the worship leader uses an illustration suggested by the culture surfers, the team members have helped to preach the gospel for that day.

Another important group is the worship team, which is made up of the people responsible for the week-to-week planning and designing of worship. At Ginghamsburg United Methodist Church in Ohio, in which the congregation has shifted to using a variety of media in worship, the celebration team is made up of the creative coordinator, the technical coordinator, the communications director, the multimedia director, the band leader, and the pastor who is giving the sermon that week. Michael Slaughter, lead pastor at Ginghamsburg, points out that it is the pastor's job to bring to the team the key idea for that week's message.[8]

While the vast majority of congregations will not have the resources to have such a team, each church should be able to identify key people who work together to create the worship experiences. Besides the pastor, the group may include a worship leader, a music coordinator, and a resource person who is responsible for the details of decorations, vestments, Communion elements, and the like.

Key leaders of the worship experience meet to focus on three issues: First, they evaluate the worship experiences of the previous week. Evaluation makes possible constant improvement and honest reflection and feedback on what is working and what needs to be improved. Second, the role of this group of leaders is to provide accountability in terms of the spiritual life of the leadership. Time for prayer, reflection, and encouragement is vital to developing healthy relationships. Third, the group engages in a creative time of planning and pulling together the various elements that make up a particular worship experience.

Worship and Spiritual Vitality

Worship is central to the spiritual vitality of a faith community. Through it, newcomers and visitors determine the heartbeat of the congregation. Public worship is for more than just believers; it is the point at which the gospel intersects with the world. Worship is the unique place where people experience the living God in community for the purpose of serving others. This experience is not just for insiders; instead, it is a witness to the community at large of what the faith community believes, practices, and is called to do as it hears the call to transform the world through the power of Jesus Christ.

Your worship team may want to read *Contemporary Worship for the 21st Century: Worship or Evangelism?* by Daniel T. Benedict and Craig Kennet Miller (Discipleship Resources, 1994), which gives practical illustrations of six basic formats of worship and ideas for how to plan worship. You also may want to read Robert E. Webber's book *Planning Blended Worship: The Creative Mixture of Old and New* (Abingdon Press, 1998), which provides an excellent historical overview of worship and shows basic formats of worship that are currently in use.

Endnotes

1 Reprinted by permission of Harvard Business School Press. From *The Experience Economy: Work Is Theatre and Every Business a Stage,* by B. Joseph Pine II and James H. Gilmore; pages 39–40. Boston, MA, 1999. Copyright © 1999 by the President and Fellows of Harvard College; all rights reserved. Used by permission.

2 See *Paul: Apostle of the Heart Set Free,* by F. F. Bruce (Grand Rapids, MI: William B. Eerdmans Publishing Company, 1977), pages 291–92.

3 Reprinted by permission of Harvard Business School Press. From *The Experience Economy: Work Is Theatre and Every Business a Stage,* by B. Joseph Pine II and James H. Gilmore; page 165. Boston, MA, 1999. Copyright © 1999 by the President and Fellows of Harvard College; all rights reserved. Used by permission.

4 From "The Very First Canela Worship Songs: How a Brazilian Tribe Learned to Sing to God," by Randy Bishop, in *Christian Reader,* July/August 1998, page 41. Used by permission.

5 From "The Very First Canela Worship Songs: How a Brazilian Tribe Learned to Sing to God," by Randy Bishop, in *Christian Reader,* July/August 1998, page 41. Used by permission.

6 From "The Very First Canela Worship Songs: How a Brazilian Tribe Learned to Sing to God," by Randy Bishop, in *Christian Reader,* July/August 1998, page 38. Used by permission.

7 From *Planning Blended Worship: The Creative Mixture of Old and New,* by Robert E. Webber; page 21. © 1998 Abingdon Press. Used by permission.

8 To see one way a church created its worship team, see *Out on the Edge: A Wake-Up Call for Church Leaders on the Edge of the Media Reformation,* by Michael Slaughter (Nashville: Abingdon Press, 1998), pages 77–78.

WHAT IS SUCCESS?

Kaunas, Lithuania, 1997

In 1944, the Soviet Union took over the property of the Kaunas United Methodist Church in Lithuania. For more than fifty years, the building had been used for many different purposes. For the last fifteen years, it had been used as a Ping-Pong hall. After Lithuania gained its freedom, Christians were allowed to have their churches back. In August of 1997, the first district meeting of Lithuanian United Methodists in fifty years was held at the newly opened Kaunas United Methodist Church. All remains of religious oppression were gone; the faith community had returned to its home.

Starting new faith communities is not something for the faint-hearted. Just look at what Paul went through in his ministry. After the rioting caused by the silversmiths of Artemis, Paul had to leave Ephesus. His whole ministry was a spiritual battle against those forces that sought to overcome him.

After leaving Ephesus, he gathered together the leaders of the Ephesian faith community in a nearby city. His final thoughts to them are a witness to us of why we undertake this task in the first place:

> I did not shrink from doing anything helpful, proclaiming the message to you and teaching you publicly and from house to house, as I testified to both Jews and Greeks about repentance toward God and faith toward our Lord Jesus. And now, as a captive to the Spirit, I am on my way to Jerusalem, not knowing what will happen to me there, except that the Holy Spirit testifies to me in every city that imprisonment and persecutions are waiting for me. But I do not

count my life of any value to myself, if only I may finish my course and the ministry that I received from the Lord Jesus, to testify to the good news of God's grace.   (Acts 20:20-24)

For Paul, success meant being faithful to his call to preach the good news of God's grace. His focus was on spreading the Word so that Jews and Greeks alike could come to faith in Jesus Christ.

Underneath the methods and the process for starting new faith communities, there must burn a deep passion for those who do not know Jesus Christ. It is this passion for ministry—this deep connection with God's desire to bring people into relationship, this conviction that without Christ, people have lost out—that fuels Christian ministry. Methods can go only so far. Plans can do only so much.

As you approach the development of new faith communities, do so with your eyes on Jesus Christ. This counsel may sound quaint or old-fashioned, but the reality is that God is the One who gives the growth. Our job is to prepare our hearts and our souls for God's work in our midst. In the Book of Acts, Pentecost started when the disciples and the women who followed Jesus met together in the upper room to pray.

It is through prayer, through gathering together with fellow believers, and through honest seeking after God's will that vision for ministry arises. With a vision comes a passion for reaching (with the gospel of Jesus Christ) particular people groups in the community—people for whom a faith community is uniquely equipped. God gives the gifts for ministry that are needed and brings individuals into the ministry at just the right time.

Faith, then, lies at the heart of this whole enterprise—faith not in our own abilities, but in God who calls us to follow wherever God leads.

Grace and Health

In 1944, the Soviet Union took over the property of the Kaunas United Methodist Church in Lithuania. For more than fifty years, the building had been used for many different purposes. For the last fifteen years, it had been used as a Ping-Pong hall.

After Lithuania gained its freedom, Christians were allowed to have their churches back. In August of 1997, the first district meeting of Lithuanian United Methodists in fifty years was held at the newly opened Kaunas United Methodist Church. All remains of religious oppression were gone; the faith community had returned to its home.

A year later, a discussion took place about how to get youth into the church. One person made a radical suggestion: "Why don't we put a Ping-Pong table in the church?" This suggestion opened old wounds in many people's hearts, especially those who had witnessed their church being turned into a sports hall instead of a place to worship God. Some in the group made the observation that many of the youth in the community knew this building only as a place to play Ping-Pong. By letting them come back to play, the congregation would have an opportunity to share the gospel. Finally, they decided to bring back Ping-Pong tables, but not in the sanctuary.

On the week the Ping-Pong table was put in, it was announced that people were welcome to come and play. Loni, a woman in her seventies, was one of the original members of the church. She had experienced the devastation of seeing the church taken away and the joy of seeing it reopened for worship. Many expected her to stay away because of the bitterness of those long years of persecution. But Loni was the first person to sign up to play, even though she had never played a game of Ping-Pong in her life. Loni, who had put her life on the line during the days of persecution, was able to bring healing and wholeness to the congregation by putting her feelings aside and witnessing to the importance of reaching out in the name of Jesus Christ, no matter the personal cost.

Perhaps we all can learn a lesson from Loni. Faith does not come without a cost. For fifty years, she had watched her church being defiled. But the faith community never gave up. The church was not the building; the church was the Christian faith community that continued to pray and worship and serve in the name of Christ, even without a building to call their own. It was that understanding of what Christian community is all about that gave Loni the freedom to play Ping-Pong that night.

As we are called to be in ministry in the faith communities to which we belong, let us take courage in the God who sustains us and calls us to live in grace and true freedom. Success is not measured in brick and mortar, nor determined by the numbers; rather, success is seen in the nature of our relationship to God and to one another. Faith is seen in our willingness to give so that others can live.

Today, the church is in the midst of great challenge and great opportunity. Like the church in Ephesus, it is called to be in ministry to many different people groups that surround its local congregations. Jesus' words to the church in Ephesus serve as a reminder and a challenge to each of us:

But I have this against you, that you have abandoned the love you had at first. Remember then from what you have fallen; repent, and do the works you did at first.   (Revelation 2:4-5)

Our passion for ministry starts with our love for God and neighbor. When we forget this basic foundation of our faith, we lose our purpose for ministry. But when this passion becomes our reason for being, nothing can separate us from the love of God, who calls us to be in ministry in this new day.

Appendix

For more information and resources related to the material covered in *NextChurch.Now,* visit http://www.umcncd.org/nextchurch.html. This Web page contains links to other resources and information for both new-church starts and existing churches. It also contains helps for district superintendents, annual conference staff, and denominational leaders as they build a system for starting new churches. In addition, this Web page has information about upcoming seminars and learning opportunities for creating new faith communities.

Resources

The General Board of Discipleship

Staff in the area of congregational development at the General Board of Discipleship are a resource for training and equipping leaders for new congregational development and for existing churches that need help to create new faith communities. Working with annual conferences of The United Methodist Church, the staff focuses on the areas of developing small groups, new worship services, and discipleship systems. For more information, call 877-899-2780 or visit the Web site (http://www.gbod.org).

General Board of Global Ministries

Staff in the area of congregational development at the General Board of Global Ministries specialize in demographics, loans, and building design. Working with annual conferences, the staff provides leadership in identifying and developing a process for starting new churches. For more information, call 800-UMC-GBGM (800-862-4246) or visit the Web site (http://www.gbgm-umc.org).

Joint Committee on Congregational Development

The Joint Committee on Congregational Development of The United Methodist Church is made up of congregational development staff from the General Board of Discipleship and the General Board of Global Ministries. The Joint Committee offers a number of opportunities for leadership training for new-church developers, conference staff, and district superintendents, as well as an ongoing national School of Congregational Development that is held at least once a year. For more information, go to the Web site (http://www.umcncd.org).

Tips for Starting New Churches and New Faith Communities

The following tips are specifically for the new-church planter. If you are starting a new faith community by adding a new worship experience in your existing church, please apply those things that fit your situation.

Before You Begin

■ Attend at least one seminar on new congregation development and read books related to the topic.

■ Visit churches that have been started recently. Ask the pastors and leaders in these churches about the process they used to start their church.

■ Attend as many worship experiences as possible in a wide variety of churches to get a feel for what makes for an effective worship experience.

■ Start at least one new small group in the church to which you belong. Better yet, start a small-group discipleship system to help you and others in the group develop a life of prayer and Bible study and to develop healthy relationships between members and their families and between members of the group.

■ Start a new worship experience or be part of a group that plans ongoing worship that specifically focuses on reaching new people in the community.

■ Pay attention to your health. Physical, emotional, mental, and spiritual health are vital tools for the new-church developer.

■ Get in touch with your creative side. Learn to play a music instrument, sing, do graphic arts, take drama classes, dance, or paint. Most successful church developers are able to think from an artistic viewpoint. Remember, art speaks to the heart.

Identify the People Groups in Your Community

1. Use the following questions to survey the people who live in your community. Pick out a neighborhood and go door to door. Or set yourself up in front of a grocery store and invite people to participate in the survey. Plan to conduct at least one hundred of these surveys yourself. (Note: If a person answers yes to the first question on the survey, thank him or her and proceed to the next person or house.)

   Community Survey
   a. Are you active in a local church?
   b. What keeps people from attending church?
   c. What is the greatest need in this community?
   d. What advice would you give to me as a pastor (or as a new-church starter)?
   e. Would you be interested in finding out more about our church? If so, please write down your address and telephone number. (For another version of these questions, see pages 190–91 in Rick Warren's book *The Purpose-Driven Church: Growth Without Compromising Your Message and Mission*.)

2. Visit other churches in the area to see what kinds of worship experiences are being offered. Look for what is working, what is not working, and what is not currently being offered.

3. Get a demographic printout of your community. Your annual conference should have access to this kind of information. The Board of Global Ministries offers churches a demographic survey. You may contact their office at 212-870-3840.
   Percept, a company that specializes in demographics, is used by many United Methodist annual conferences. Contact your conference denominational staff to see what they can provide and how to best use demographic sources for your church start.

4. Drive and walk around in the community to see what fits and what does not fit with the demographic picture.

5. Talk to key leaders in the community. Find out where future growth will take place, what is happening in the public-school system, what the most important needs are, and what opportunities are available to be in service.

6. To discover the normative pattern of where people go, check out traffic flow on work days and at the time you are planning to offer your first worship experience. For example, if you are in a rural area and a Wal-Mart opened in a central location, plan to place your church nearby, because that's where many people will want to be on the weekend.

Develop a Healthy Core Group

A healthy core group is a Christian community that supports, prays, and works together as a team.

1. Design your discipleship system. Develop or find a resource that you will use for developing the core group of your new congregation. Develop the ongoing classes or experiences that will be offered to help people grow in spiritual maturity.
2. Formulate the core values, mission, and vision for ministry of the church.
3. First meetings and events tell people your purpose and lay down the genetic code of what this faith community is going to become. Start everything with prayer.
4. Design first gatherings as the first part of your discipleship process.

Find an Appropriate Meeting Space

Decide on the space you will need for gathering and what you will need for office space and small groups. For large gatherings, the following sites offer good space:

1. Schools: It is better to use a high school or middle school, because high- and middle-schoolers may feel as if they are regressing when worshiping in an elementary school.
2. Warehouse
3. Strip malls
4. Movie theaters, dinner theaters, or playhouses

Make sure you have meeting space for music rehearsals and a room for childcare.

Obtain Equipment

Obtain the following equipment:

1. Computer and color printer
2. Telephone answering machine
3. Music system
   a. Public-address system. Make sure you get one that can handle electric keyboards, guitars, and bass guitars as well as vocals.
   b. CD or cassette player. Music can be played as people enter or for solos.
   c. Keyboard with MIDI. (MIDI means you can connect your keyboard with another keyboard or a computer.) A professional

keyboard can play organ music as well as piano and a wide variety of instruments. Look to spend about $1,000 and up for a professional-quality instrument.

d. Drum set (for a church that plans to have a praise band). Your best bet, if you can afford it, is an electric drum set, because you can adjust the volume to fit the size of the room. You are more likely to find a drummer if you provide a drum set.

4. Overhead projector and screen or an LCD projector and screen. LCD projectors cost about $5,000, but prices are going down with more widespread use. LCD projectors connect to computers and can project Powerpoint presentations to use for singing or announcements. (Be sure to get appropriate permissions for projecting music or words to songs. See the section below for information about obtaining permission.) LCD projectors can also be connected to a VCR for projecting videos.

Obtain the Necessary Licenses

You will need at least the following licenses:
1. Christian Copyright Licensing International—for printing or projecting words of songs. Call 800-234-2446 or visit their Web site (http://www.ccli.com).
2. Motion Picture Licensing Corporation—allows you to show video tapes in worship. Call 800-462-8855 or visit their Web site (http://www.mplc.com).
3. Also check the worship section of the Web site of the General Board of Discipleship (http://www.gbod.org).

Assemble the Staff

1. Getting the person responsible for the music onboard is a top priority. The kind of music you offer will determine who comes.
2. Look for an administrator who will help you coordinate the growth of groups and ministries in the congregation.

Develop a Budget and Financial System

1. Develop a budget for the first two years. Plan to share this task with your core group and with denominational staff who are working with you.
2. Develop a process for receiving funds. Ask the treasurer of the district or annual conference to handle and process funds until you are well enough established to have your own treasurer.

3. Look for opportunities to share your vision for this new ministry with people who would be interested in helping to fund the work. Ask other churches or individuals to buy specific pieces of equipment for the project. Develop donors who will begin to see this as part of their giving ministry.

Launch the Public Ministry

1. Have a discipleship system in place before you start.
2. Develop a worship team to provide support and leadership for worship.
3. Lay out the themes and Scriptures for the first ten weeks of worship.
4. Offer the first worship experience when you are assured of at least 120 people in worship. Some congregations develop a small-group system of from eight to ten groups and bring them together for the first time at the launch. Others do phone marketing or mass mailings. Many do a combination of the two.
5. Consider the style of your worship service. Style of worship is determined by the people you are trying to reach.
6. Determine a dress code. The way worship leaders (musicians, greeters, speakers, liturgists, ushers) dress communicates to worshipers what is considered acceptable dress in worship.
7. Make sure the people who lead the service represent the same people group you are attempting to reach. A diverse leadership for the worship service (musicians, liturgists, and speakers) suggests that a diversity of people are welcome.
8. Have a dress rehearsal of the service the week before it is offered at the site.

Take Care of the Children

1. Offer quality childcare and church school for children. Contact the The United Methodist Publishing House (800-672-1789, ext. 6167) for free church-school material for new congregations.
2. Develop a system for registering all children who attend church school. Why not provide laminated, numbered cards to keep track of parents and children? The parent picks up a numbered card when he or she drops off the child and returns the card when picking up the child.
3. Develop a discipleship system for children and youth.

Have a System for Following Up on Visitors

1. When someone visits the church, follow up with a letter from the pastor and a visit or phone call from a lay member of the church. Develop a system to tell whether visitors are returning. If they are not coming back, try a different way of following up, or change the people who are making the contacts. Keep careful track of people as they come and of their response to your ministry.

2. Develop a registration card that includes a box to identify if a person is a visitor, an attender, or a member. (An attender is someone who attends on a regular basis but has not become a member.) Have a box on the card for prayer concerns and for interest in classes or ministry opportunities. (For a great example of a registration card, see page 261 in Rick Warren's book *The Purpose-Driven Church: Growth Without Compromising Your Message and Mission*.)

3. Develop a newsletter to keep visitors, attenders, and members informed.

4. Print business cards with the name, address, telephone number, and Web address of the church on the front and a map of where your worship service is held on the back.

5. Invite people to join small groups, Bible studies, and ministry opportunities.

Take Care of Yourself

1. Develop an accountability group of which you are a member.

2. Create a prayer group of people outside your ministry to keep you and your ministry in prayer.

3. Find a mentor—someone who has started a church in the past— whom you can call for advice and support.

4. Communicate to the congregation which day is your day off each week and which day you do your sermon and worship preparation. If you hold to these days, people will respect your time.

5. Protect your family time.

6. Pray daily for guidance and wisdom.

Tips for District Superintendents and Denominational Leaders

Attend a School of Congregational Development

Every year the Joint Committee on Congregational Development offers specific training for district superintendents and conference leaders. Leaders go through the basics of how to create and support new churches and how to help turn around existing congregations. (See page 167 for more information about the Joint Committee.)

Build Leadership Rather Than Buildings

The old model of establishing churches was to have a district buy a piece of land, appoint a pastor, and then help the pastor build a building. Today, annual conferences are finding success by investing in the leadership first. A well-trained, motivated church planter will establish a church that will buy its own land and build its own building.

Some annual conferences are finding success in establishing Academies for New Church Development. After identifying clergy and lay leaders to be trained, the annual conference pays the cost of training. Annual conferences and some jurisdictions have been setting up their academies, with a goal of creating a pool of leadership for new-church starts.

When a church planter is appointed, the annual conference sends that person to the School of Congregational Development for focused training on the steps to take to establish a new church. Annual conferences have also been sending to these schools pastors and laity of existing churches that are looking to turn around their existing ministry. Pastors who are newly appointed to these churches are good candidates for this training.

Appoint Strong Pastors

Early in the appointment process, think of who you are going to appoint to the new church so that he or she can have time to prepare and receive training. Better yet, establish a pool of trained pastors out of which new appointments can be made. You need the most well-balanced, creative pastors for this task. Do not appoint a pastor who is having marital problems or other personal issues that will keep him or her from giving the new-church start his or her full attention.

Appoint for the Long Haul

Appoint pastors who will make a commitment to the new church for eight to ten years, if not more. A long-term pastorate at the beginning helps to establish a healthy, strong congregation.

Do Not Start Worship Too Soon

Support the new-church planter by giving him or her the time to establish a core group and enough people in a small-group system to ensure that more than 120 people will be at the first worship experience. In some cases, this may take more than a year. This is the most important step in creating new-church starts. It is hard to recover from a first worship experience in a public launch that does not go well or does not attract enough people to get it over this first growth barrier. If a core group is unable to gather enough people for the first worship experience, don't launch. Re-evaluate the situation before proceeding.

Buy Enough Land

It used to be the rule of thumb to buy from three to five acres of land near a well-traveled road. Today, the rule of thumb is to buy from fifteen to thirty acres, which will allow the congregation to develop into a regional church. For churches to grow, they need parking and room to grow.

When Land Is Expensive

Look at rented facilities in a strip mall, a business park, or a warehouse area. Or buy a supermarket or similar building that has closed, and retrofit it for a church.

Do Not Build Too Soon

Once worship starts, the natural tendency is for congregations to want to have their own building. But churches that build too soon can severely limit their growth potential. When a worship experience maxes out its space, encourage the church to add worship experiences.

Go to http://www.umcncd.org for online helps for district superintendents and conference leaders. The site contains ideas and insights for developing new faith communities.

Reproducible Pages for Leadership Development

You have permission to photocopy the worksheets, graphs, and diagrams on pages 177–91 to use as you share the ideas in this book with other leaders in your congregation. To use these materials in other settings, you must obtain permission from the Discipleship Resources Editorial Offices: P.O. Box 340003, Nashville, TN 37203-0003, phone 615-340-7068, fax 615-340-1789, e-mail mgregory@gbod.org.

Reproducible pages related to Chapters 1 through 4
1. Community Profile
2. Discovering People Groups

Reproducible pages related to Chapters 5 through 7
3. Vision for Ministry
4. Pastoral Leadership in an Existing Congregation
5. Leadership Core Group
6. Core Group Vision
7. Structure for the Twenty-First-Century Ministry System
8. What Is Your Discipleship System?

Reproducible pages related to Chapters 8 and 9
9. Settings for Congregational Life
10. Dynamics of Groups Settings and Settings for Ministry Survey
11. Ministry, Strategy, and Structure

Reproducible pages related to Chapter 10
12. Worship Matrix
13. Identifying and Using the Theme
14. Worship as Drama

1. Community Profile

Past Population	Current Population	Future Population
10 years ago	Now	10 years from now

% of Population

Ages	Past	Now	Future
18 & Younger			
19–30			
31–50			
51–65			
65+			

% of Population

Racial-Ethnic	Past	Now	Future
White (non-Hispanic)			
Black			
Hispanic			
Asian			
Pacific Islander			
Native American			

2. Discovering People Groups

Church	Community
Worship Attendance (Last 10 Years)	Population Growth (Last 10 Years)
Ethnic Makeup	Ethnic Makeup
Age Groups	Age Groups
Lifestyle Groups (families, singles, and so forth)	Lifestyle Groups (families, singles, and so forth)
Needs of People	Needs of People
Greatest Problem	Greatest Problem
Go to **http://www.umcncd.org/nextchurch.html** for a church survey.	

3. Vision for Ministry

■ **What is your vision for ministry?**

■ **What is God calling you to do that may be different?**

■ **What people group(s) are you going to reach for Christ?**

■ **What practices and beliefs will characterize your faith community?**

4. Pastoral Leadership in an Existing Congregation

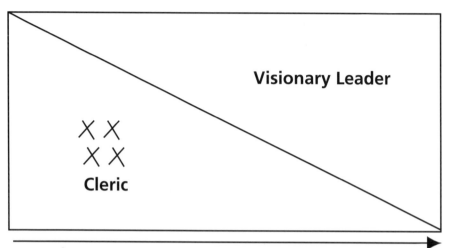

Years in Appointment

5. Leadership Core Group

■ Is your pastor seen as a cleric, a visionary leader, or somewhere in between?

■ What is the history of your church in relationship to this question?

■ How is your congregation developing a healthy core group?

■ To what spiritual disciplines is the leadership core committed?

■ How are you developing healthy relationships?

6. Core Group Vision

As you develop a core group for a new faith community, ask:

What resources do you bring as a core group?

■ **Call**

■ **Spiritual Gifts**

■ **Talents**

■ **Passions (Who do you want to reach and why?)**

■ **Leadership Styles**

7. Structure for the Twenty-First-Century Ministry System

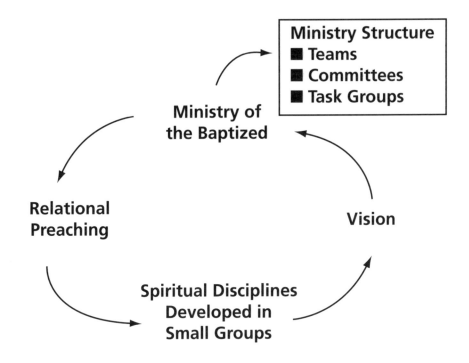

8. What Is Your Discipleship System?

■ What is happening in the lives of people who are now (or will be) participating in the life of your congregation?

■ What would you like to have happen in their lives?

■ What are the essential beliefs of the Christian faith?

■ What are the spiritual disciplines to which your members are committed?

■ What is your process of discipleship for new people coming into your church?

1st year	2nd year	3rd year	4th year	5th year

9. Settings for Congregational Life

SMALL GROUP (5–15)	FELLOWSHIP/ INSTRUCTION (50–80)	CELEBRATIVE WORSHIP (120+)
Practicing spiritual disciplines	Everyone knows your name	Glorifying God
Focused on personal growth	United by single focus	United by worship experience
Diversity found in multiple groups	Homogeneous cultural perspective	Diversity accepted, as there is room for everyone

10. Dynamics of Group Settings and Settings for Ministry Survey

Dynamics of Group Settings

Number in Group	Setting	Results
4	Personal Interaction	Perfect for personal interaction and close-knit discussion. (Jesus, John, James, and Peter)
5–15	Small Group	Perfect for discipleship and accountability. Large enough for continued interaction and support. (The Twelve Disciples)
16–49	Floundering	Group struggles for self-identity and longs for the former intimacy of the small group.
50–80	Fellowship/Instruction	Self-sustaining group that is homogeneous and single-focused. Perfect for instruction and teaching. (70 Disciples)
81–120	Awkward	Size group where people long for the easy familiarity of the fellowship group size.
120+	Celebrative Worship	A large-group dynamic takes place that enables people to focus on God.

Settings for Ministry Survey

Settings for Ministry in Your Local Church	■ Identify groups in your church that match these groupings. ■ Do they fit the description? ■ How could they be reconfigured to better match their best use? ■ Do you have a good balance of small group, fellowship/instruction, and celebrative worship?
4 (Personal Interaction)	
5–15 (Small Group)	
16–49 (Floundering)	
50–80 (Fellowship/Instruction)	
81–120 (Awkward)	
120+ (Celebrative Worship)	

11. Ministry, Strategy, and Structure

■ How are you developing a healthy core group?

■ What is your process of discipleship? What is it for yourselves? for existing members? for new members?

■ How are you incorporating the primary task in your ministries?

■ What is your ministry system?

■ How will you work together (teams, committees, task groups, and so forth)?

■ What are your current ministries? What changes, deletions, reshaping, or new ministries are needed?

12. Worship Matrix

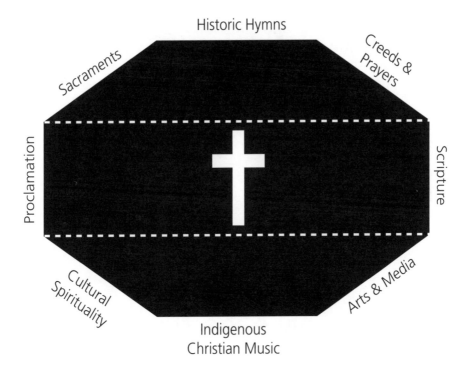

- ■ **Proclamation: casting the vision for the faith community**

- ■ **Sacraments: Lord's Supper and baptism**

- ■ **Historic Hymns**

- ■ **Creeds & Prayers: Apostles' Creed, Lord's Prayer, and so forth**

- ■ **Scripture: Old and New Testaments**

- ■ **Arts & Media: drama, dance, choir, graphics**

- ■ **Indigenous Christian Music: the music of the people**

- ■ **Cultural Spirituality: from the culture, redeemed in worship**

13. Identifying and Using the Theme

■ Identify the theme and question based on Scripture.
(Theme: "Through faith in Jesus Christ, your life has
purpose" 1 Corinthians 9:24-27.)
(Question: "Does your life have purpose?")

■ Identify the indigenous motif (running a race).

■ Find media (drama, video, song, story, and so forth) to
raise the question (scene of runners in the movie *Forest
Gump*).

■ Find media (drama video, song, story, and so forth) that
echoes the theme ("Thy Word").

■ Develop a sermon that responds to the question.

14. Worship as Drama

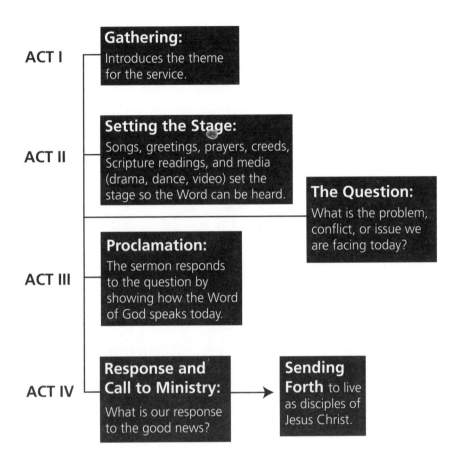

ACT I — **Gathering:** Introduces the theme for the service.

ACT II — **Setting the Stage:** Songs, greetings, prayers, creeds, Scripture readings, and media (drama, dance, video) set the stage so the Word can be heard.

The Question: What is the problem, conflict, or issue we are facing today?

ACT III — **Proclamation:** The sermon responds to the question by showing how the Word of God speaks today.

ACT IV — **Response and Call to Ministry:** What is our response to the good news?

Sending Forth to live as disciples of Jesus Christ.